Also by Robert John DeLuca

Novels:
The Pact with the Devil
The Master of Deceit

Non-Fiction:
The Perfect Pro Football Coach

Beatles, Books, Bombs, and Beyond

Beatles, Books, Bombs, and Beyond

Robert John DeLuca

Throughout this book the author has tried to recreate events, locales, and conversations from his personal memories of them. In a very few instances in order to maintain anonymity, names of individuals have been changed. Otherwise, all characters, incidents, and dialogue are real and not products of the author's imagination. Since the actual conversations in the book occurred over fifty years ago, those presented are based upon the author's best recollections. Given this extended period of time it would be impossible to recount conversations on an exact word-for-word basis. Rather, the author has provided them in a way that evokes the feeling and meaning what was said, while striving to ensure that the essence of the dialogue is accurate. The description and accounts of certain events, where the author may not have been present are based upon written research, reports, interviews, and discussions by and with third parties, who are deemed to be reliable. The author endeavored to report only facts with respect to the description of actual events and does not offer any opinion whatsoever as to underlying causation associated therewith. The author's intent is strictly to relate his story as seen through his eyes as impacted by his direct interaction with people and events described herein.

ISBN: 1542998085
ISBN: 13:9781542998086
Library of Congress Control Number: 2017902045
CreateSpace Independent Publishing Platform
North Charleston, South Carolina

This book is dedicated to those guileless young men and women who proudly answered their nation's call in the 1960's and went off to war in Southeast Asia. Many never returned. Few of those that did received even a thank you from the folks back home.

If I had some more time to spend
Then I guess I'd be with you my friend
If I needed someone.

"If I Needed Someone" by George Harrison, December 1965

Contents

Introduction

THE BASEBALL GAME ITSELF HAD been pretty unspectacular that night in the Astrodome a few years before the Y2K fizzle. I couldn't tell you who won or even who the Astros played. The game had just ended, and we were seated behind home plate while the field was being converted for the real reason we had showed up. My wife, Joyce, and I sat there and took in the expanse of the "Ninth Wonder of the World," which was the first domed stadium anywhere when it opened in 1962. The arched network of girders, spectacular exploding scoreboard, brightly colored seats, and AstroTurf were all getting a little tired by then, but the place was still impressive. Hey, the Dome was the '60s; *we* were the '60s!

Our reverie was short-lived. Owen, our oldest of four sons, all of whom were with us, squirmed and twisted in his seat. "C'mon, let's get out of here!" he whined. "I wanna go home!"

An immediate vote of support came from Warren, son number two. "Yeah, let's go! I don't want to watch a bunch of old people dancing around." Marshall, the next in line, decided his best tactic was to take off down the aisle steps, screaming as he went. The youngest, Graham, who was certainly a party to the cabal, feigned sleep to further, I suppose, convince his parents how exhausted he was.

Over the three hours or so, we had stuffed them full of Coke, popcorn, cotton candy, chili dogs, and whatever else they peddled there at that time. Food bribery was probably not going to work now. I had to resort to reasoning, a tactic which also was seldom successful. "Look out there," I said as I pointed toward second base, where a crew was hastily assembling a stage. "The Beach Boys will be out there very soon. They are really good. You will like them! They are kind of like Sean Cassidy." Our mutineers were unimpressed. Sure enough, Mike Love and his gang trudged out and after only a song or two, the collective commotion of the 15-, 13-, 10-, and 7-year-olds once again prevailed. So much for "Good Vibrations." Kids! We had no choice but to turn our backs and walk out on that incredible band formed in 1961 and quash some of our fondest memories of that implausible time to have been alive.

As a baby boomer just on the cusp, I ratcheted into manhood during that most impressionable decade of my life when so much happened so fast that it is almost impossible to believe that it really all occurred. Just think about it: the moon landing, the Beatles, Vietnam, Martin Luther King, feminism, the Great Society, free love, miniskirts, civil unrest, Cuban missiles, Fidel Castro, MLK assassinated, JFK assassinated, RFK assassinated, Elvis, Woodstock, Cassius Clay, and, of course, the Beach Boys. America was never the same. As a college student and military officer candidate during this remarkable time, I found myself living on an Ivy League campus that was becoming inundated with a flood tide of free expression and burgeoning liberalism. At the same time I was becoming personally immersed in the United States Marine Corps, one of the deepest pools of traditional and fundamental conservatism anywhere. I had a choice: go with the flow or try to swim against it. Even then I understood the gravity of my decision. My choice might even cost me my life—as it did for many of my fellow students, including two of my most precious friends.

My life had begun to pick up speed in late 1962 when I strolled onto the Brown University campus in Providence, Rhode Island, for the very first time as an incoming freshman. I had been raised in a comfortable middle-class home just forty short miles to the north in Massachusetts. Although I wasn't sure what to expect, I knew that I was about to set foot on a whole new path that would irreversibly change things forever. I got it. There'd be no looking back. I was leaving the nest and had better be able to fly away on my own. What I did not foresee, nor could perhaps anyone have foreseen at the start of the 1960s, was just how dramatic and rapid a transformation our society, our country, and indeed the entire world was about to undergo. Much of what I had come to accept and believe was turned upside down and inside out. It was a tough enough struggle for a young guy to find where he fit in without also having to deal with this rapid societal makeover. Somehow, I made it. I am still here. Heartbreakingly, though, some of the best and brightest are not.

By any measure, I have enjoyed a wonderful existence over the past five decades. Joyce and I have raised four terrific, if occasionally annoying, sons, all of whom have beautiful families of their own and are successful, accomplished professionals. While there have been a few bumps in the road, as diminishing strands of the gray hair leave my head and the moss accumulates on my back, I can look back on a life chock full of love, pleasure, and satisfaction. Still, I am troubled by one persistent thought that will haunt me, I am certain, to the grave. It is really quite simple: why me, Lord? Why was I spared when others, who may even have deserved to live more than I, were taken?

I know I can never answer that question, but I have decided it is time to tell my story about the parallel lives and interrelationships of two pals and myself. We were born in the '40s, raised in the '50s, and levered into manhood during the unbridled '60s. Despite my staunchest intent to report events and discussions as they actually occurred, some of my observations and recollections herein are no doubt altered, shaded, and made fuzzy by all the years that have flown by since those star-crossed days. We were fun-loving, serious, naive, immature, and yet mostly dependable, all in one package. We studied, played sports, partied, drank beer, chased girls, horsed around, fell in love, graduated, got married, had kids, and two of us died.

Although we arrived at Brown in the fall of 1962 as strangers, we came from similar backgrounds and shared many common expectations and beliefs. As fate would dictate, the three of us were thrown together as classmates, athletes, and Naval Reserve Officers Training Corps (NROTC) candidates. It was inevitable that fast friendships would emerge. For the first four years, we scribed matching paths across the university landscape, attending many of the same classes, playing on the same sports teams, attending summer military cruises together, and frequently partying in the same groups. After graduation, we became United States Marine Corps (USMC) second lieutenants at precisely the same instant, and then trudged down to Virginia for real basic training. A year later, two of us ran off to flight school in Florida, while the other stayed on the ground at supply school in North Carolina. While our career paths diverged, our ultimate destinations did not: Southeast Asia and the Republic of Vietnam. We all went. Only I came home.

CHAPTER 1

The Bell Tolls

IT WOULD BE A STRETCH to say that we were the best of friends. Heck, we each ended up joining a different fraternity. On the other hand, we were good friends. We did not have the sort of relationship where one person was compelled to immediately call another to share the details about the latest woman in his life or, later on, even to brag about kids and family. But like it or not, our lives were virtually locked in parallel for the better part of the wildest decade in recent US history. We went through a lot together, even though our social circles and daily routines were often very much apart. All that said, we genuinely liked and respected each other. One of us might not see another for a while, but at the next meeting, the conversation would pick up where it left off. It just so happened that our lives meshed together in college during the very critical transition from adolescence into adulthood. We were boys who were becoming men, and tough Marines at that. Even after getting our degrees and moving on to new locations, we knew that our paths would cross. Sooner or later, somewhere, we'd meet up over a beer—until, of course, two of them were gone.

There is nothing to document with absolute certainty the exact moment Jerry Zimmer, Charlie Pigott, and I met, but if it wasn't at the NROTC building, old Lyman Hall on the Brown University campus, it had to have been on Aldrich-Dexter Field at freshman football practice.

1

It was mid-September 1962, and Coach Charles Markham had assembled his latest group of potential gridiron talent. As an "Ancient Eight" institution in the Ivy League, whose members took pride in a sense of lofty academic achievement, Brown, in recent times at least, had seldom distinguished itself in a positive way on the football field. In fact, the season before we arrived on College Hill, the Bruins had gone "0" for the schedule, when they racked up a total of twenty-four points to the good and two hundred forty-five to the bad. The team was shut out five times in nine games, and never scored more than nine points. Our newest group, however, was supposed to be different. University bigwigs were set to celebrate the institution's bicentennial in two years, and rumors had it that an extra concerted effort had been underway to bring in some decent football players.

After hearing about this alleged drive to upgrade the program, I had to wonder just how big a "push" could have been made. Sending recruiting letters to the mediocre high school players like me hardly seemed indicative of an effort to beef up the squad. The very first day, though, as I stood there in uniform with Charlie, Jerry, and about fifty others and looked around at the motley group of players as Coach Markham addressed the squad for the very first time, I pretty much conceded that my playing days were numbered. As remote a college football backwater as Brown may have been, there was no question that there were indeed more than a few very talented athletes on hand. In fact, fifteen of the guys out there had been captains of their high school teams. Quarterback Bobby Hall eventually became the fifth-round draft pick of the Minnesota Vikings. Billy Peters, who was also to become a USMC second lieutenant, started for several seasons as a defensive back. Both Charlie and Jerry, who came from Binghamton and Williamsville, respectively, had been excellent high school players in upstate New York. Charlie, who was a tight end and a pretty big and tough-looking guy, did play a lot as a freshman, and no doubt would have been successful on the varsity in later years. Jerry was decidedly rugged and hard-hitting, but just was not the hulking monster that the coaches favor. He became relegated to the position of backup guard and linebacker, and like many of us, never did particularly distinguish himself on that freshman team.

I had played in the Bay State League in Massachusetts, which was the second highest of the four classes of high school football in the state. As a senior, I had started at center for a winning team. In those days, with that background, one might have expected that I might be able to find a place in the depth chart of a program that just lost every game in one of the least competitive college football conferences. Well, that roster spot on the freshman team turned out to be perhaps sixth string on a good day. As things worked out, none of us three, who had all performed with some distinction on the gridiron in high school, played football again after our freshman year. It was time to hang up our cleats and direct our energies in more productive, self-rewarding pursuits that didn't come with so many bumps and bruises. Personal preferences aside, in Charlie's case for sure, and perhaps also with Jerry, the Brown bicentennial team definitely could have used their contributions.

Even at a place like Brown where, to bastardize a thought from Vince Lombardi, "academics are the thing, the only thing," the game of football is an emotional undertaking for those involved in it. Just to be out there requires a big-time psychological commitment. Competitive fires must burn somewhere. Comparisons to the military are inevitable and immediate. In combat, all squad members face the real prospect of having to undergo shared periods of duress, which are sometimes followed by occasional bursts of elation. In football, there is a similar instilled sense of comradery that runs deep and can be very appealing to an alert, optimistic young man ready to take on the world. In other words, if you like playing football, there is at least a chance that you would consider it fun to run around in the dirt with a rifle. The fact that all three of us had played the game may well have been a driving factor that led us to seek a place with the self-declared best fighting force in the world. Hey, you have to be tough, with no sense of quit, to play football. That sounds a bit like the USMC, doesn't it?

Looking back on my abbreviated involvement in college football, I do recall one very special moment, which occurred during one of the first freshman practices on Saturday, September 22, 1962. It was an unusually hot and blustery afternoon in East Providence. Summer had hardly made an exit, and not even the leaves on the trees hinted that fall was coming soon. It should be no surprise to anyone that a university that had been around for 200 years was replete with a hodge-podge of traditions and historical precedent. Brown was certainly no exception.

On the edge of the main campus overlooking College Hill there is an impressive concrete-and-brick structure known as the Carrie Tower. It is located perhaps a mile or so from the football practice field where we were standing. While I haven't ever bothered to look it up, I assume that campanile is named for some long-otherwise-forgotten benefactor who shelled out some cash. Based on the amount of alcohol that flowed on that campus in those days, it seems unlikely that it was named for prohibitionist Carrie Nation.

Nonetheless, as the custom hewed over the decades dictated, the bells in this noble structure are only to be rung on two occasions: at commencement, and upon a football victory. As a consequence, it seems likely that the bells themselves must have been getting quite rusty back in the early 1960s. Commencement was a pretty sure bet, but don't plan on hearing much in the fall. Not quite so fast, ye of little faith. Coming off the 0-9 disaster in 1961, the 1962 version of the Brown team marched resolutely off to Hamilton, New York, that afternoon to face the Raiders of Colgate in the opening game.

As the new freshman team stood there that afternoon and listened to Coach Markham prattle on about formations, strategy, studies, drinking, and of course, blue darters (more often referred to as "flatulence" by

Ivy Leaguers), a nervous excitement unexpectedly rippled through the team. Charlie Pigott, whose short-term attention span was often notoriously apparent, was the first to react. Ignoring the coach's monotone, he turned to Jerry standing next to him. "Hey, what was that? Did you guys hear that?"

"Hear what, Pigott?" Jerry responded.

"Wait a second! Listen. There it is again. I hear it too," I chimed in.

"Yeah, so, what is the big deal?" Jerry snapped back. "Just some church bells. It must be four o'clock or something."

Suddenly, Charlie got it. He stammered out, "It is the Carrie Tower bells that are tolling! Don't you know what that means, Zimmer? They won! The varsity actually went up to Colgate and won a game. That hasn't happened around here since forever!"

By that time, the entire squad was buzzing. Even Coach Markham stopped his monolog. He removed his ball cap, scratched his head, and smiled. Everyone standing there at that moment knew that something special had just happened. The disastrous previous year was all but forgotten; *our* varsity Bruins had gone to upstate New York and kicked the Red Raiders' tail by a resounding score of six to two. The slumbering Brown football program, of which we were now a part, had suddenly awakened from hibernation, or at least rolled over in the cave. As things turned out, that win at Colgate was the only one they would get that entire season, but the timing of that single triumph was incredible. There were big grins all around. It really was a terrific way to start off a college career.

CHAPTER 2

Charlie, Jerry, and Bob

IF BY CHANCE BACK IN the early 1960s you happened to have spent a lazy autumn Saturday afternoon in a bar watching football with a group of guys you hadn't previously met, including Charlie Pigott and Jerry Zimmer, it is very likely a week later you would distinctly remember both of them. Each would have made an impression on you, but for entirely different reasons. You'd recall Jerry as friendly, likeable, and smiling often, even though he came across as somewhat reserved and subdued. At the same time, he still conveyed a quiet confidence. When he spoke, it was usually worth listening. Hardly shy or reticent, Jerry was clearly a deep thinker who considered well what he said before he opened his mouth.

On the other hand, when he chose to participate, Charlie just naturally tended to dominate any conversation. Not a huge man, but possessing the rugged, physically imposing frame of the tight end that he was, Charlie had a way of expressing himself in clear and non-negotiable terms that left little question where he stood on any issue. He was not afraid to take a position and defend it, if necessary. He was loud, to be sure, and almost brash, but not quite. As outspoken as he could be at times, he was deeply intelligent, and hardly ever jumped into a conversation without having thought about it first. Charlie was bold, but not impetuous. While he could be domineering, Charlie was not a braggart or loudmouth in any

7

sense. He was naturally garrulous and enjoyed being around people. While sometimes it was tough to get a word in edgewise, nonetheless he was easy to like. He truly cared about those who mattered to him.

Charles William Pigott

Charles William Pigott arrived in Providence in the fall of 1962 having graduated from Williamsville High School in upstate New York, not far from Buffalo. At some point, his family relocated to York Town Heights in the very tony Weschester County, just north of the Big Apple. Charlie never acted like he came from money, but more like a solid middle-class kid from comfortable circumstances, but who still understood the need to work hard to achieve success. There was no sense of entitlement in Charlie. I am certain that from an early age, Charlie must have been a very active child who gave his parents all they could handle. Surely, much of his boundless energy must have been channeled into outside activities, especially team sports. He had to have been a bright student, whose grades were consistently good. As was the case at Brown, and later in the Marine Corps, people tended to gravitate toward Charlie. He had a wonderful gift of possessing natural leadership qualities.

By the time he was ready to move on to Brown, he stood a couple of inches over six feet and tipped the scales in excess of 200 pounds. He had a rock-solid build, and had excelled on the gridiron at Williamsville High. Apparently he had played well enough to attract the attention of the Brown's head football coach, John McLaughry, who put forth a concerted effort to attract him to Providence. Charlie's Navy scholarship award and an assured place in the Brown NROTC unit helped convince him to enroll at the Rhode Island school. I suspect that, given his academic achievement, football prowess, and overall high school credentials, Charlie probably could have pursued a number of other alternatives had he chosen not to come to Providence.

In many ways, Charlie Pigott was the whole package. He was a terrific student, possessed a natural congeniality, and excelled as a gifted athlete. As if those qualities were not enough, he was tall and boyishly handsome. His light-sandy-brown hair that was almost blond helped to set off his piecing blue eyes that seemed to bore through you when you had his attention. His smallish nose was offset with a more than adequate mouth, which he was seldom reluctant to use. His complexion was fair, and he had soft features on a face that was constantly expressive and sometimes a dead giveaway of what he was thinking. His close-cropped hair (i.e., Navy, USMC, and the times) and well-toned body gave him an impressive and distinctive appearance. It was hardly surprising that he would be attractive to the ladies on campus. In fact, fairly early on he began dating a fellow student who was to become his wife.

Charlie tended to stand out in a crowd. He had a natural charisma about him that was readily apparent to everyone around him. He approached every task with a unique aura of self-assurance and confidence. When Charlie moved forward, he didn't have to look around to see if people were following, because they just naturally seemed to be there. It was not surprising that he was elected president of both his fraternity, Phi Gamma Delta, and the Semper Fidelis Society, a student USMC organization. Even more impressive, he was chosen in his senior year to be the company commander for the entire Brown midshipmen corps. His strong leadership qualities were openly manifest on many occasions throughout his time at Brown.

It was fun to be around him when he got excited, which was quite often. There appeared to be few things in life about which he was truly neutral. As his Marine orientation firmed up through the years, he did not hesitate to mock the Navy personnel, whom he irreverently referred to as "squids" most of the time. He was loud, and he was gruff. Sometimes he would get so excited over something that he would stammer and have trouble getting it all out. On those occasions, he liked to fire short, staccato blasts. Everyone in the area needed to take cover. His sense of humor was incredible, and he could find something to smile about in almost every situation. He was well grounded, and never took himself too seriously. When joking, he never was reluctant to call artillery fire right down on his own position.

External bravado notwithstanding, Charlie also had a deeply reflective and thoughtful side. He firmly believed in the United States of America and maintaining our proper place in the world. He was dedicated to serving his country as a United States Marine, and did not have a lot of time for those who protested against everything for which he stood. There were no bounds for his love for his family. And yet, even though he could often come across as obdurate, uncompromising, and with little time for anyone who disagreed with him, Charlie had a tender spot a mile wide when it came to true friends. He was willing to do almost anything for a buddy, and did. He would always be there for someone in need. It didn't matter if he hadn't seen you for one day or several years, his warmth was immediately apparent. You always could count Charlie. The bluster and pomp some people associated with him was just really a thin facade. It was a tragic injustice that he was swept from the face of the earth at such a tender age. You had to love Charlie, and I did.

Jerry Allen Zimmer

The first thing I ever heard about Jerry Zimmer was that he grew up among the cows on a dairy farm in upstate New York. Quite often, folks from the country are inevitably connected to farms, tractors, cows, chickens, and pigs, whether or not they ever knew the north or south end of an animal. In Jerry's case, though, I am pretty sure that during his youth he had used a bucket and stool every now and then at four in the morning. I know just enough about cows to recognize that they must be milked every single day. I don't think there is a button to turn off mother's milk.

There are no weekends, holidays, or time off. A dairy farmer must be dedicated and all-in for the duration. The Jerry Zimmer I knew certainly possessed those ingrained qualities of persistence, reliability, and determination, which he clearly acquired in early childhood. If Jerry decided to get involved, it was all the way.

While Charlie was loud and naturally gregarious, Jerry was much more reserved and measured in his approach to most things. He operated with restraint when it came to opening his mouth. He was not one to jump up and lead the cheers, at least until he had studied all aspects of a situation. Once he was in, though, he wasn't one to vacillate. He was a man of strong convictions and exhibited absolute loyalty to those people and causes where he chose to be involved. Jerry could sometimes give the impression that he was "all business," with little time for anyone or anything other than his own strictly defined agenda. In reality, however, that was hardly the case. He was at heart an open and friendly guy who enjoyed people, and got on well with most everyone. He was not the boat rocker that Charlie could be. He preferred to take his shots on his own terms. As a lightning rod, Charlie had his detractors and advocates, but I would be surprised to find anyone who didn't like Zim.

The community of Maine, New York, is located a few miles northwest of Binghamton along the southeastern border with Pennsylvania. The most widely known reference point is the nearby Greater Binghamton Airport, which serves the proximate region of the Empire State. Jerry was the oldest son of the Elma and Warren Zimmer, who also had two other boys; Jim and Jeff. Jerry's dad, Warren "Zim" Zimmer, owned a dairy farm, and indeed young Jerry did spend considerable time growing up and working in and around the barnyard. Despite the demanding nature of farming, Jerry didn't seem to mind, and had pleasant memories of his youth. While Jerry was not physically imposing, he had a wiry and robust build that was at least in part, I am sure, from having tossed many a hay bale from ground to truck to barn. He was an excellent student at Vestal High School where he starred in football, wrestling, and lacrosse.

When Jerry decided on Brown, he became one of the first young men in the area who would attend a four-year university. His interest in the school was very likely prompted by the iconic nearby IBM Corporation in Endicott, New York, one of the area's "triple" cities. Chairman Thomas J. Watson, "a Brown man born and a Brown man bred," as the song goes, was a consummate alumnus promoter. His open affection and avocation for the school helped elevate Brown to high profile in southern New York. As a well-rounded and excellent student, Jerry might well have been directed toward Providence at the suggestion of his high school guidance counselor, who was familiar with Mr. Watson's advocacy.

His subsequent service as a Marine pilot in combat further embellished Jerry as a cherished local favorite son. In high school, Jerry had already developed a strong interest in flying for the Corps. He and his chum, Gene Mares, often fantasized about one day actually being USMC pilots. In fact, both achieved their aviation goals and actually flew missions together in Vietnam. Gene, on occasion, was Jerry's "rear seater," Radar Intercept Officer. Jerry was honored posthumously with the naming of Zimmer Field, which has become the center of little league and other youth sports activity in Maine and the surrounding area.

As football players, Jerry and I shared the same fate at Brown. While he was much more athletic than I was, neither one of us possessed the large, bulky bodies that coaches favor for lineman. Jerry may have approached five-ten, but was surely well under six feet. At the most, he carried some 185 pounds or so on his farm-hardened, athletic frame. At Brown, he kept his copious light-brown hair almost wavy on top but always closely trimmed on the sides. His somewhat square-shaped face with high cheekbones may have been traced way back to the eastern European origins of the Zimmer name. His thick eyebrows accented his hazel eyes. While Jerry tended to run deep, he was not reluctant on occasion to intentionally test the waters with ludicrous statements. Such remarks tended to surprise those around him, unless you knew to catch that slight mischievous twinkle that quickly flashed in his eyes.

Jerry's practicality and hardscrabble upbringing also shone through in other areas while he was at Brown. To say that he was thrifty was an understatement. He had obviously learned the value of a dollar growing up, and wasn't about to waste a penny if he didn't have to. I am by no means implying that he was not generous and giving by nature, because he certainly was. There was no question; in any time of need, he would be by your side. On the other hand, if you lent him a sawbuck until Tuesday, Tuesday might not come for a while. You'd always get paid back in full, but it was not in his nature to throw money around. It probably would have been very difficult for Jerry Zimmer to have realized his dream to attend Brown University without the full regular NROTC scholarship that he had earned.

When I think back about my personal relationship with Jerry Zimmer today, some fifty years later, a couple of images come to mind. The first is a crystal clear recollection of him on the lacrosse field. I can look at old team photos, but even those don't quite capture the essence of him for me. I can still see him sauntering gracefully down the field, cradling the ball high back and forth in the wicket of his stick, which he is holding in gloved hands. He is decked out in a white helmet with a metal face guard, a gray sweatshirt with the sleeves ripped out, and light-brown shorts. His powerful legs and muscular calves are pumping over floppy, drooping white socks that refuse to stay up. His is the picture of health, youth, and athleticism. He is determined to put the ball in the goal.

It also strikes me how strong-minded he could be, most often in a very positive way. Failure was simply not an option and never occurred to him. I had never played lacrosse before. I doubt if I had even picked up a stick. The game looked like fun, but in my deliberative Yankee way, I wasn't sure I could master it, and probably would make a fool of myself trying. Jerry had played the game for years and was obviously pretty good at it. When I asked him about going out for the freshman team he was very encouraging. He assured me I'd be cradling the ball like an old Iroquois Indian in no time. He knew I would pick up the game very easily. There was no hesitation in his voice. He was absolutely convinced that it was the right thing to do for me. His counsel certainly helped, and I did play for three years. I only wish that Jerry's optimism and my capabilities had meshed a little better on the field. Nonetheless, I am very happy to have participated, and have Jerry Zimmer to thank, at least in part, for getting out there.

I have been very fortunate in my life to have been touched by many, many, wonderful and devoted friends. I have been much closer, frankly, to some than I ever was to Jerry Zimmer. On balance, though, I can think of few people in my life that I truly admired as much as Jerry. From my vantage point, the guy really had his act together. He came off a farm and quickly adjusted to one of the most competitive academic environments around. He chose a path for his life and never wavered. He was consistent, focused, and determined to get where he was going. And yet, he still managed to be a terrific friend, wonderful husband and father, resolute patriot, and downright great guy. Jerry Zimmer had little pretense about him. I am certainly a better person for having crossed his path.

Robert John De Luca

And what was I up to while those two New Yorkers were baling hay and wooing the girls and scoring touchdowns on the high school gridiron? Well, I was raised about twenty miles west of Boston and less than fifty miles north of the Brown campus in Framingham, Massachusetts, once an old New England mill town that was already feeling the effects of the burgeoning growth of nearby Boston. I was the oldest of the four children from a pair of Class of 1940 Brown graduates, John DeLuca and Barbara Porter. Naturally, I was very aware of the school during my entire childhood and had pretty much set my sights on Providence early on. My father was a civilian employee at the US Army Labs in nearby Natick, and my mother was an elementary teacher for a number of years.

We arrived in then semi-rural Massachusetts from ultra-urban Providence in 1952 and moved into a modest, three-bedroom, ranch-style house with a dirt driveway and no garage in north Framingham. For me it was an emancipation. Cork ball in the street became real pickup baseball in a cow pasture. We had no trouble finding "material" for bases. An occasional few hours of fishing with my father in a waste-polluted mill stream became after-school jaunts with a can of earthworms down the hill to "pristine," or so it seemed, Lake Cochituate, less than a half-mile from my house. "Butchie" Guslowski, my very best friend in Providence, was replaced by new best friend "Bunkie" Otenti. In fact, it was under a forsythia bush in our front yard one evening that my new, apparently much more erudite friend, gave me my first lessons in the facts of life. I dismissed it all as pure bunk at the time. Had we not moved, I have no doubt that Butchie would have eventually given me the same lesson in the city, albeit probably under a bridge near the railroad tracks.

We had only one car and, of course, a party-line phone. Bunkie and I remained fast friends up until our high school years when we drifted apart. His father was a bookmaker; not the bindings and covers variety. Bunkie was not college material, although he was never at a loss for ways to get ahead. In fact, while I was at Brown, Bunkie came up with an unusual request. He asked me to "sit in for him" on an electrician's union aptitude test in Boston. The things we do for friends! I was lucky I didn't get caught and have electrodes attached to my private parts. As I expected, I never heard anything further from him about becoming an electrician. Sadly, he died tragically a few years later, when his Corvette could not negotiate a turn and slammed into a tree.

My formative years were spent in decidedly middle-class circumstances, where we lacked for little but were by no means well off. My parents resolutely believed in higher education and were determined to send their entire brood through college, even though they knew that it was going to be a challenge to educate four children on a civil service salary. I was always a decent, if not quite superior, student, who was good at everything and poor at nothing. Although I truly excelled at very little, I always was blessed with a strong work ethic and the fruits of my labor generally were rewarded. "Work hard and you shall be rewarded" was still in vogue, way back then.

Sports have always been a focal point of my life. I played football in high school with some degree of success, even though baseball was my first, though unrequited, love. In the winter, I spent hours clearing snow off ponds after school to play hockey, only to have it come down again before we could get around to actually playing. I was diligent and persistent, if not too practical. In 1960, when the American Football League was formed, my father purchased 10 shares at $5.00 per share of stock for me in the Boston Patriots, making me, by my judgment, an original NFL owner. The current group does not seem to agree. I loved the Boston Bruins, who never won anything, and hated the Boston Celtics, who won championships every year. So much for my judgement.

It would be exaggerating somewhat to say that my father's general philosophy was only slightly right of Attila the Hun. Personally, I have always considered myself much more enlightened in my beliefs and preferences, yet decidedly more conservative than progressive. Recently, a sister-in-law in Maine challenged my political bent, "What ever happened to you since you left Massachusetts and moved to Texas?" I do not believe anything has. As a high school senior I was never quite comfortable with our neighbors, the Kennedy clan, but hardly advocated the other side, either. My high school buddies, including Harry Potter (his real name, no fooling) and I were taken by JFK's charisma, to be sure. Harry and another friend, Steve Larrabee, and I spent countless hours riding around town checking out the DQ and other gathering spots, looking for girls while debating where our lives were headed. It is amusing to me to recall that every so often in those conversations the Marines would come up. The Marines was sort of the most extreme alternative to college. "Screw it all! I am just going to join the Marines!" was echoed a time or two by all of us. I never, ever, at that time, thought that I would really do it. Steve shuffled off to Amherst, and Harry became a prominent Boston attorney after graduating from Wesleyan and spending a tour in the Special Forces.

Many of my immediate relatives had served in the Armed Forces in WWII, including my father as a lieutenant in the Coast Guard. In 1962, the military as a profession was still held in very high regard, and I was more than eager to pursue the NROTC scholarship, which I was fortunate enough to win. Without it, UMASS or Northeastern may have been more viable and affordable alternatives for me. At the time, I was delighted with the idea of a Navy commission. The USMC was hardly on my radar screen at that point. In fact, as he was with many things, my father was dead set against the Corps. I am not really sure why.

I set off for Brown from a relatively unremarkable family background, armed with a confirmed work ethic and enough flexibility (or maybe confusion) to pursue opportunities as they unfolded. I admired those folks such as Jerry Zimmer, who knew where they wanted to go right from the start.

We three young guys were among the three dozen or so of our classmates who opted for the NROTC program. Coming from similar backgrounds and sharing common circumstances at Brown, it is not surprising that Jerry, Charlie, and I became good, if not close, friends. The four years flew by, and we became second lieutenants at precisely the same time. We were all to have wives and children. We all were resolutely convinced that what we were doing was right. We all shared tremendous regard and affection for our families, our country, and the United States Marine Corps. While I am not absolutely certain, I am very confident that our personal ranking of those three priorities was quite similar. We all went to Southeast Asia. They went as pilots, and I as a ground officer. Now, as I enter my seventh decade of what has truly been a marvelous life, my regret is more manifest than ever that those terrific guys never made it even to their third.

CHAPTER 3

Finally Off to College

TWO HARDLY EARTHSHAKING EVENTS MARKED the start of September 1962. In England, some long-haired dude named Ringo Star replaced Pete Best with the Beatles, and I began my studies as a full-fledged Brunonian. When the big day finally arrived, my mother, father, and I loaded my newly purchased tan plastic suitcase, with imitation brass top snaps that kept popping open, and other assembled motley possessions into my father's green '56 Chevy station wagon and headed south from Framingham toward Providence. Just like that, I was finally really "off to college." Back then, however, there were very few interstates, and most of this trip took us through the center of several struggling manufacturing towns like Ashland, Hopkinton, Woonsocket, and Pawtucket.

As we drove up College Hill and approached the Brown campus, I felt a little like Jed Clampett arriving at Beverly Hills. I actually was fairly lucky that the Chevy was only six years old and still reasonably presentable. It was virtually pristine by my father's standards. He never quite bought into the American romance with the automobile. Cars were way, way down his priority list. In fact, he later owned a gray Dodge and lost a hubcap from the left front wheel. After searching the local junk yards he could not find the proper replacements. To solve this dilemma, he purchased two used matching but entirely different hubcaps and put them on the left side so that each side of the car had a different set of hubcaps. Problem solved. It is not possible to see all four wheels at the same time. Yankee ingenuity? Thriftiness? We'll stop right there.

Littlefield Hall was situated within the original main campus and had been constructed long before anyone gave much thought to automobile traffic patterns. It was positioned perpendicular to George Street, which was very busy with through-campus traffic. We had to double park and toss my gear onto the sidewalk while Dad hunted for a parking space somewhere nearby. While Mom and I waited, I was able to take in the building that was to be my home for most of the next twelve months. From the outside, if you were into Ivy League and old New England stuff, it perfectly fit the part. Littlefield Hall was built in 1925 and had undergone the constant rigors of four decades of student assault. It was a long, dark-red brick three-story rectangle with white painted wooden trim around the windows and doors. Of course, most of the brick was hidden beneath thick clumps of ivy vines that smothered all the exterior surfaces. The ancient John Carter Brown Library and old Episcopal church flanked the dorm along George Street on the west and east, respectively. Aesthetically at least, so far, I was getting what I expected. And did I mention that it was almost directly across from the dining hall? Huge plus.

After a few minutes, Dad came walking up grumbling under his breath. I can only imagine where he left the car. We picked up my things and entered my new digs. The three of us were less than overwhelmed by the spartan appearance of the place. I was on the first floor at the end of a narrow, stark corridor with drab, blue walls and a painted concrete floor. My room itself was surprisingly spacious, with two each wooden desks, closets, metal beds, and large windows. The ceilings were at least eight feet high. The walls were in reasonable shape except for several paint chip spots up toward the ceiling. Heck, lead-based paint did not become dangerous until almost fifteen years in the future.

There was, of course, no AC, and the heat was provided from old cast iron hot-water radiators. In order to sleep on many nights you had to deal with a cacophony of banging pipes. (I suppose that was good military training.) The bathrooms were down the hall near the front door. My roommate had been there but was out when we arrived. I glanced at his luggage tag: "South Bend, Indiana." Wasn't there a pretty big school closer to home for him?

As luck would have it, both Jerry and Charlie ended up only a few steps away in Hegeman Hall, which was a very similar Littlefield and also one of the original dorms on the campus. Almost all the older buildings in this part of the campus had had plenty of time to acquire the requisite ivy that flourished on the exteriors. Unfortunately, creative young men on their own for the first time can come up with many ways to amuse themselves in order to put off cracking a book for just a few more hours. A decidedly poor choice of pastimes at a place like Brown is to try to burn the ivy. Such practice is most assuredly frowned upon by the administration, and campus cops don't like it much either. A couple of Littlefield freshmen found out about that the hard way. No, *that* prank did not involve any of us.

Okay, so now we had seen my room, such as it was. What next? My parents were headed across town to Cranston, where they would visit my father's sisters. The thought of mouthwatering Italian food, a given at their house, was tempting, but I begged off with the excuse that I needed to unpack and settle into my room. Even though logic was not necessarily my father's strong suit, especially during periods of emotional stress, which for him seemed like most of the time, in this case I was able to prevail. Standing there on the sidewalk outside the dorm, the moment had finally arrived. I promised to write (remember, this was 1962). We looked briefly at each other, and they turned away to find the car. I didn't dare show emotion; it wasn't allowed in our family.

It is worth taking just a moment here to briefly discuss a phenomenon that has universally applied to every first-year college student everywhere, and no doubt has existed even before Brown was founded some 200 years ago. In most instances, even though both parents and student have been anxiously anticipating "going off to college" for at least a year or two, consummation of the actual act inevitably gives rise to long-suppressed emotions that suddenly bubble to the surface.

There are few situations in life that tug on the heartstrings more acutely than dropping off your child at their dorm for the first time and then having to drive home alone. Watching that pitiful, tiny waving figure shrink and finally disappear in your rear mirror is akin to outright misery. The excitement and anticipation are over, and it finally hits you that things have changed forever. That little kid in diapers is gone, like it or not. Outwardly parents bravely struggle to espouse thrill and delight, but when the deal is finally done, at least for a while, the stark reality of the loss hits home hard.

It also cuts both ways. Though they would never admit it, the most anxious-to-get-away son or daughter must also deal with these pangs of sadness after Mom and Dad have driven off. Fortunately, the incoming student has so much to deal with that there is scant time to dwell on the melancholy.

While homesickness can be pervasive among new students, we were far too preoccupied in coping with everything that was being thrown at us to dwell very long on what used to be. Plus, among all the gravity and seriousness associated with being on our own for the very first time, it is easy to forget that, basically, we were still, by and large, fun-loving kids. After all, we were supposed to be bright guys, and knew that having a good time trumped most other things. Although we had come to Brown from an array of locales and family situations, few of us had, up to that point in our lives, been faced with the stark realities such as feeding hungry mouths, paying mortgages, or dealing with serious disease.

All that was to come. We knew that we had to figure out this college life stuff, but we weren't interested in tackling all the world's problems yet. Just because we now lived in Littlefield or Hegeman Hall instead of on Elm Street did not mean we had leaped into maturity overnight. Hell, the truth was that we were still just kids at heart. Growing up was just about to start.

CHAPTER 4

Welcome to Brown University

I HADN'T BEEN AN IVY Leaguer for more than a few weeks on a Sunday evening in early October. There was a brisk breeze, and tendrils of leaves swirled around the bench where I was sitting on the college green in the middle of the main campus. My father had just dropped me off and was headed back home to Framingham, which was an hour or so ride. I had made my first and totally uneventful trip home for the weekend, but inexplicably, as I walked across campus toward my dorm, I was seized by a wave downheartedness. I missed my home, my parents, my siblings, my high school friends, and all the things in the comfort zone I had now left behind. I knew it would soon pass, but for a few minutes, I struggled to control the lump in my throat and abject feeling of loneliness that had overwhelmed me out of nowhere.

In the gathering darkness, as I fought to regain my composure, I found myself gazing around at the cluster of ancient buildings and diverse architectural styles set within abundant greenery and century-old trees that lent character and perspective to the world-class reputation the place had justly earned through the years. For the very first time I felt a sense of the true magnificence of Brown University. Established in

1767, the institution would soon celebrate the 200th anniversary of its founding, which predates this country by almost a decade.

Eventually my eyes came to rest on the oldest structure at Brown, University Hall, which was constructed in 1770. It is a modestly imposing, rectangular, four-story red brick structure with a central projected section, which, I understand, was patterned after Princeton's Nassau Hall, of all places. The windows and exterior trim originally consisted of painted white cedar, and there was a copula on the roof. When it was completed, the College Edifice, as it was first known, was virtually the entire university. During the Revolutionary War, in December 1776, after the British landed troops not very far away at Newport, the building was commandeered as a barracks and hospital for American and French troops. The university, by the way, was first known as the College of Rhode Island until 1804, when John Nicolas Brown, an alumnus of the class of 1786, chipped in with a $5,000 check to get his name put on the door.

My temporary gloominess, notwithstanding, Brown University is a beautiful and delightful place. There is simply no debating that statement. A visitor walking through this area cannot fail to be impressed by the vitality of the school, despite the overwhelming aura of historical precedent. If you happen to be a newly enrolled student, chances are you feel just happy to be there. Even though George Washington only visited and did not sleep there, University Hall remains the centerpiece to this day. Located at the top of College Hill, the stately main campus overlooks the city of Providence from the east, where it blossomed and grew in the midst of a grand old residential neighborhood. Having been constructed gradually over more than two centuries, the university's buildings convey a rich sense of architectural diversity. While the traditional historic red brick, which was so popular in New England's colonial days, is in evidence, there are numerous exceptions with Romanesque, cut stone, postmodern, bold concrete, and various other styles blending together in an eclectic mix.

The original small main campus is enclosed by ornamental black iron and brick column fencing that includes the university's signature Van Wickle gates on the east side directly in front of University Hall. This sacred portal is only opened to admit incoming freshman and at Commencement, when only graduates may pass through. The northeast corner of the main campus is guarded by the magnificent Carrie Tower that is just under one hundred feet tall. Faunce House, which is Brown's answer to a student union, is also within the original campus. Tucked back toward the middle is the Isabelle Leeks Theater, which, prior to its conversion in the late 1970s, was known as Lyman Hall and was home to the Brown NROTC unit for almost three decades.

Brown has several libraries scattered about, although the primary one is the Rockefeller Library, or as the students know it, the "Rock." During our years, and I am sure it is still true today, the Rock offered an inviting refuge for students seeking a quiet place to study hidden away in the stacks and remote carrels. Incessant distractions attendant to clustered college living arrangements made it all but impossible at times to knock out required papers or cram for exams. The Rock offered a cherished academic sanctuary, but it also provided a more subtle venue as one of the more likely places to hook up with our distaff classmates from Pembroke. It was quite common back then to have "study dates" with the ladies at Brown. During our first days at the university, the infamous "parietal" rules were still very much in force. These ridiculous administrative mandates attempted to dictate student conduct, especially in the presence of the opposite sex. The Rock was a safe haven from such ridiculous impositions. Charlie Pigott, who met and eventually married a Pembroker, Carol Crockett, surely studied on occasion with her at the Rock.

Brown's campus is smack in the middle of an urban setting that was fully developed decades ago. The only new land available for the inevitable expansion has come from acquisitions of existing nearby dwellings and buildings. Brown's answer to undergraduate student housing needs consisted primarily of two complimentary monster quadrangles. The Wriston Quad accommodated the fraternities separated by upper-class, independent "buffer" dorms, and the West Quad was the home of most freshmen. Each of these complexes occupied at least an entire city block each on the south side of the main campus. The casual visitor to campus was a lot more likely to see a football being tossed around in the Wriston Quad than a Frisbee, the popular pastime over at the West Quad. By the same token, my guess is that the mass aggregate GPA over at the West Quad was quite likely several points higher than where the frat boys hung out.

Both facilities were constructed in the late 1950s and were still relatively new in the early 1960s. Neither of them, however, possessed the Ivy ambiance of Littlefield Hall, complete with the nightly banging pipe serenades. The world-renowned, gastronomical hallmark, five star-aspiring Sharpe Refectory was the primary dining campus facility and was located at the north end of the Wriston Quad.

There are sundry other classroom and academic department buildings located outside the main campus interspersed among the surrounding neighborhoods. In fact, long after we three Marines aspirants had left the scene, Brown pulled off a major "jump-shift" deal with Bryant College, whose campus was located just to the southeast. Brown traded considerable open, undeveloped acreage it owned in northern Rhode Island near the Massachusetts border for Bryant's contiguous property in Providence. Bryant then built a brand-new campus at the new location and moved everything out there. It seemed to be a great deal for both. Bryant, which did not even play football back then, has since returned the favor by beating us on the gridiron.

Brown and Pembroke students were well integrated by the early 1960s, even though the women's college was not officially merged until a few years later. The Pembroke campus was located about four blocks to the north through dense urban neighborhoods. In recent times, however, the campuses have been virtually combined into a single tract. Most Brown intramural and intercollegiate sports activities are held at the Aldrich-Dexter Fields multiplex. At "AD" you'll find the Meehan Auditorium (ice hockey), Pizzitola Center (basketball), aquatic center, field houses, football, lacrosse, field hockey, soccer, and numerous intramural fields. While this complex is located just three or four blocks northeast of the main campus, you'd best be reasonably physically fit to get out there while negotiating the kamikaze-inspired Providence motorists. Football is still played in ancient Brown Stadium built in 1925 on Elmgrove Avenue in East Providence, two miles away. Perhaps in their wisdom, the founding fathers anticipated the pigskin struggles that were to ensue and purposely made it just a bit more difficult to get out there on a Saturday afternoon.

CHAPTER 5

The "Big Me" Generation

REFLECTING BACK TODAY, OVER A half-century since we stepped onto the Brown campus as wide-eyed freshmen, feigning confidence but in fact oozing naivety, I appreciate far more than ever how really significant those years were in the molding us into men and how much the university influenced that process. What I find even more fascinating, our personal development notwithstanding, is that during that short window in the mid-1960s while we were there, the institution itself was undergoing a transition of unprecedented proportions. The very philosophical underpinnings that had survived on College Hill for two centuries were being suddenly shifted and uprooted. Stated more simply, the Brown we entered was hardly the Brown that existed a short decade or so later. Change is an expected and constant dynamic among sophisticated institutions of higher learning, but the upheaval of the 1960s was unprecedented.

Certainly, from brick-and-mortar and enrollment standpoints, the change at Brown has been ongoing and dramatic. Even though it remains ranked among the smallest members of the Ivy League, when all programs and levels are considered, Brown has grown significantly. Enrollment today exceeds some 8,500 and boasts an endowment north of three billion dollars. In the early '60s, Brown had only a little over 2,000 students, and I would be surprised if the endowment reached even $100 million. When we arrived, Brown was still "technically" an all-male place, even though the ladies at Pembroke College attended Brown classes. Everything was moving toward a fully coeducational institution, but it still didn't officially happen until 1971. Both my parents graduated from Brown, in the Class of 1940. Whether or not my mother had truly earned a degree from Brown was a frequent dinnertime topic. My father seemed to take umbrage at that notion. The Brown and Pembroke campuses were physically separate. The geographic totality of "our" Brown University was basically restricted to the main campus as it is still configured.

Physical facts and measurable statistics aside, since the great upheaval of the '60s and early '70s, I do not believe the university has changed ideologically very much, if at all. Brown has always championed individualism and the sacred right to independent thought. Those concepts have always been woven into the fabric of the school and will never change. Brown is about as liberal or progressive-minded as a university can be and still retain a decent sense of order about it to be able to function effectively in the larger, less progressively tolerant general society. This decided liberal bent was around in the early 1960s but did not seem the dominant, all-encompassing attitude that has emerged and permeates all aspects of the university community today. The decades of the '60s and '70s changed everything.

I live in Texas, where somehow a Brown alumnus, Bill O'Brien, has become the head coach of the Houston Texans of the National Football League. His ascendency to that position is another story, but as is inevitable, head coaches are constantly under heavy scrutiny from the media. Coach O'Brien's roots have been long discussed in the land of oil derricks and Longhorn herds. Enjoying a recent modest three-game winning streak, the coach was complimented for his flexibility. In fact, that positive aspect of his approach was attributed to his Northeast upbringing. His assistant coach was quoted in the *Houston Chronicle* as stating of O'Brien: "He is very flexible. He grew up in the Northeast (Boston) probably in a pretty liberal family. He went to Brown, *one of the most liberal places in the world.*" Brown has earned its reputation far and wide. On the other hand, if a Brown man can become a head coach in the NFL, maybe a C student at Yale like George Bush can even become president.

When we arrived, there was still room for many of the traditional values and even acceptance of much of the establishment aspects of our society as a whole, such as the military, that long since have been summarily ushered out of campus life. With ire and dissatisfaction with the Vietnam War as a root dynamic, Brown underwent a major transformation during the decades of the 1960s and 1970s. Almost anything and everything that represented the old guard or the status quo was summarily challenged or rejected. In doing so, the university was mostly paralleling a movement toward liberalism in US society in general, although at a much accelerated pace. When some of the most extreme Brown students were burning flags and spitting on servicemen returning home, such practices were still not pervasive throughout our entire society. Brown could have resisted, but instead willingly joined the fray. Never impinge upon the right of free expression.

In his recent book *The Road to Character, New York Times* columnist David Brooks discusses this wholescale societal evolution from a different perspective. After recounting the almost refreshing humility with which our country accepted the end of World War II, Brooks recounts what he sees as a shift from a culture of humility to what he calls "The Big Me." Our culture has been transformed to where it now encourages people to see themselves as the center of the universe. He mentions a study in 1948 wherein 10,000 adolescents were asked whether or not they considered themselves to be a "very important" person. Only 12% said yes. The same question, when posed in 2003, brought fully 80% affirmative replies. In another study in 1976, dealing with the personal importance of fame, respondents ranked it 16th out of 17 in a list of "life's ambitions." By 2007, 51% of respondents ranked "becoming famous" as one of their top personal goals. The self-effacing person in our society who is tolerant and gracious, has largely been replaced by an egoist striving for self-promotion. The humility of the '40s and '50s is all but forgotten. Many of these attitudes have been apparent at Brown for many years.

Across society, traditional barriers to long-accepted standards of behavior and norms quickly fell by the wayside. Before the real changes had begun in the early 1960s, Brown was already generally regarded as one of the most liberal schools in the nation, where alcohol flowed like water, and yet, at that time the drug scene, including marijuana, was virtually non-existent on campus. If drugs were your deal, you had to head down the Hill to the Rhode Island School of Design. By the late 1960s, however, that situation was hardly still the case on the Brown campus.

How about sexual conduct and permissibility? The archaic iron-fisted parietal rules still were in force at Brown in the early 1960s. Believe it or not, you were only permitted to have a young lady in your room from 1:00-3:00 PM on Sundays <u>and</u> *while she was there you must always keep both of your feet on the floor!* (As I have indicated Brown is a place that has always encouraged creativity.) That was Brown University in the early 1960s. With the onset of the Vietnam War, things changed almost overnight. As brand-new freshmen students in 1962, we had little awareness that we were about to be swept over the waterfall of a rapidly changing society. We had to learn to sink or swim pretty damn fast.

While the degree of change that has occurred on College Hill since the conclusion of the turbulent '60s and '70s is open to much debate, there should be little question that the place did evolve a great deal during that unique time period. The question remains just how much did this rapid transformation away from conventional morals and humility toward the "The Big Me" generation impact three young men bent on serving that very Satan-driven government to the point of sacrificing our lives? In answer to that question, I would say that we were rather fortunate to have been there as ROTC students in the mid-'60s rather than a few years later. We became increasingly marginalized as the years and war went on. Just a short time later, uniform-wearing students were ostracized to the point of open harassment. Of course, that problem was simply solved by the faculty and administration by banishing all military programs from the campus. Had Jerry Zimmer, Charles Pigott, myself, and several of our classmates been on campus a few years later during those embarrassing times, I am absolutely certain that our attitudes and convictions toward service to our country and the United States Marine Corps would not have waivered.

CHAPTER 6

Where the Heck
Is Vietnam?

As I HAVE DISCUSSED, THERE little question that our society has undergone a wide-ranging transformation since the early 1960s. Societal
evolution notwithstanding, however, typical American youths must still
confront the daunting task of negotiating their way out of adolescence
and into adulthood. Such issues must be dealt with by both sexes, and
few periods of life are more challenging than having to deal with the
rites of passage that are fraught with endless strings of ups, downs, elation, and despair.

As the country emerged from the somewhat sedate and stable 1950s,
few in the mainstream of society could have predicted just how rapidly
and radically our culture would change in just a few years. By and large,
most children were raised in intact nuclear families who lived and played
together in placid and wonderful cities and towns across America. The
kids participated in Little League, saluted the flag, prayed in the classroom, and were taught that hard work and perseverance inevitably led to
good things. The world was a much larger place. Books and magazines
offered our best glance of what lay beyond our shores. Radio was the
electronic marvel of the day, with television just beginning to become an
ingrained familial focal point. Newspapers were still king and were the

primary source of current events. Computers hardly existed. There were no cell phones, Internet, or even Super Bowl, for that matter. World War II had ended long ago, although as a nation we were over licking our wounds from the "police action" in Korea. The American dream was flourishing, and as the new decade broke, life in these United States was as stable as it had ever been.

As the class of 1966 invaded the Brown campus in the fall of 1962, few of us in that heterogeneous group of young people had really dwelled very much on what was in store a few short years ahead. We eight hundred or so very bright young men and women were far more concerned about discovering paths into adulthood, and were becoming increasingly anxious to get there. And as if that quest alone was not enough, we were perceptibly tossed headlong into a fomenting university community. Most of us were away from home and on our own for the first time. Overnight we shed the restrictive shackles of parental supervision and shockingly found ourselves guided only by our own unbridled self-determination. No one made us study, go to class, or really do much of anything. Fortunately, for most, common sense and rational behavior prevailed, and we were able to make necessary adjustments to succeed. Many of our classmates, however, simply could not handle this parental emancipation. Freedom proved to be a curse, and they were gone in just a semester or two. Sadly, in most instances, the high first-year attrition rate had little to do with innate academic ability.

The period of adjustment to campus life, especially at Brown, where individual liberty was hallmark, was perplexing and arduous to most. No one should have been surprised by the rigors of acclimating to academic life (i.e., "the books") at an Ivy League institution. The grade grind, which was tough enough, was expected. What we didn't anticipate, however, were the implications of ominous clouds that were building on the world stage. The eventual resulting storms would soon send shock waves back through our society and be particularly impactful on university campuses. The world outside of Brown University that we were destined to enter underwent an upheaval that would leave it far different than we had been expecting.

There seems little debate now that the Vietnam War was the singular, overriding dominant event during the decade of the 1960s and 1970s. In looking back, however, as the decade opened, I am surprised to recall how relatively insignificant that issue was. To the general public it was far below the horizon of US international affairs, but not for long. An enchanting and dynamic president pumped with panache, style, and new ideas had entered the White House in 1960. He replaced the steady-as-you-go ex-general, who had proven to be the perfect caretaker for the affluence and growth the country enjoyed over the latter half of the decade of the '50s. President John F. Kennedy had done little more than shed his inauguration tux when he was confronted with a swelling paranoia about the spread of dreadful, hated communism, particularly in Latin America. In an ill-fated attempt to deal with this sinister threat and on the advice of his closest advisors, in April 1961, JFK authorized the Bay of Pigs invasion into Cuba. The disastrous results of this CIA-inspired brainstorm are well documented. Partly as the result that abject failure, which was somehow designed to overthrow Fidel Castro, Russian Premier Nikita Khrushchev sensed he had detected a vulnerability in this new, green American president. He reacted swiftly and quickly, and convinced Castro to permit his Russian nuclear ICBMs to be positioned on Cuban soil, only 100 miles or so from South Beach in Miami.

In September 1962, just as the wide-eyed Brown class of 1966 were moving into their dormitories, US intelligence sources confirmed the presence of the Soviet nukes. Pandemonium prevailed, and Kennedy faced a crisis that even dwarfed the Bay of Pigs boondoggle. The hawkish Joint Chiefs of Staff urged the president to launch a full-scale invasion, which they felt was the only solution. The days became so tense that in an unprecedented move, parts of the US military were raised to the alert status of DEFCON 2, which is thought to be the highest level of alert status ever implemented, including to the present day.

On October 22, 1962, a tenuous Kennedy addressed the country on national television. Resisting tremendous pressure from his military chiefs and many members of Congress for a stronger response, he announced an immediate blockade of Cuba and quarantine of all Cuban military goods. Furious back-room negotiations ensued and on October 27, a deal was struck: Kennedy agreed to remove missiles we had positioned in Italy and Turkey in exchange for Russia's removal of the missiles in Cuba. An outright guns and bombs confrontation had been narrowly averted. The United States had been teetering on the brink, but cooler heads prevailed.

As I stood in the crowded dorm room of Senior Proctor Larry Gross at Littlefield Hall and watched events unfold on his blinking black-and-white television, I shared a profound sense of relief with everyone around me. One had to wonder, however; if such a negotiated outcome had not been reached, might we brand-newly minted NROTC midshipmen have been immediately called to active duty? Perhaps we had just dodged a bullet and didn't even realize it.

Unfortunately, we were not to be so lucky with South Vietnam. Even though I lived through every agonizing month of it, I can still hardly believe that US military presence in that out-of-the-way, far-distant backwater mushroomed from virtually zero to a peak of 536,000 troops in a very short period of time. The "off-the-radar" conflict when the decade started soon reared its ugly head and snatched away the headlines, never to relinquish them. It is doubtful if many of us midshipmen had thought very much about serving in Southeast Asia during our last couple of years of high school when we took the Navy scholarship exams. I know I didn't.

As had been the case in Cuba, our government had adopted a staunch Cold War foreign policy based upon "containment of the spread of communism." While JFK had sensibly pulled up just short of an open shooting confrontation in Cuba, he was nonetheless on board with the basic containment approach. In fact, he was very concerned that our recent stumbles at the Bay of Pigs and the Berlin Wall had damaged our international reputation among friends and enemies alike. It was his judgement that the United Sates could not afford another failed attempt to gain control and thwart communist aggression, where the price would be another damaging loss of credibility on the world stage. He began to focus on Southwest Asia for an opportunity for us to regain favor, and decided that Vietnam would be the ideal place for us to take a stand against communist takeover. How hollow that thought rings today.

Apparently as the result of shoddy intelligence or a gross miscalculation on our part back in 1961, the United States somehow opted to put our faith in the Vietnamese leader, Ngo Dinh Diem. We backed him on the assumption that his forces could and would defeat the communist guerrillas on their own. Kennedy, to his credit, clearly did not want to send US forces there in large numbers and sincerely hoped that Diem would prevail. The dismal quality of the South Vietnamese military, however, soon dictated otherwise. Diem's leadership and his forces proved so inept that the United States stood calmly by in March 1963 when a group of generals overthrew and executed the man we had stringently supported. With Diem gone, Kennedy began to gradually increase troop strength in RVN. At the time of his tragic assassination in November 1963, just after we had begun our sophomore year on College Hill, US troop strength stood at sixteen thousand, up from the two-thousand level of 1961. There had been nine hundred advisors under Dwight Eisenhower. Historians have argued back and forth about whether or not this escalating trend would have continued had Kennedy lived. No one can say for sure. On the other hand, there is certainly no debate on the actions of his successor, who slammed the hammer down, and US involvement on the ground skyrocketed.

When Lyndon B. Johnson took over on November 22, 1963, it seemed at first that he would continue to concentrate where he had spent the bulk of his time; in the Congress, dealing with domestic affairs and continuing to push for the imposition of his "Great Society" programs. Up to that point, the newly empowered Texan had not shown a whole lot of interest in the war.

An interesting side note is that President Johnson actually made an appearance at Brown in 1964. I attended his speech at the Meehan Auditorium. Little of the substance of his remarks remains with me, although I do distinctly recall his lazy Texas drawl. I cannot imagine him showing up on campus a few years later. Great Society hot buttons aside, LBJ very soon became irrevocably committed to increasing our commitment to the war. In August 1964, our destroyer, the USS *Maddox*, was attacked in the Gulf of Tonkin by what were thought to be North Vietnamese torpedo boats. This overt act of outright aggression against US forces in international waters led to the Gulf of Tonkin Resolution, which authorized the president to conduct military operations without officially declaring war. The proverbial fox was now in the hen house. It was all Johnson needed to be off and running.

During these early years of the conflict, the strength of guerilla forces, which came to be known as the Vietcong, had been steadily mounting to the point where as early as 1964, a force of some one million had been assembled. LBJ and his minions just could not seem to get it right as one tactical blunder followed another. The bombing attacks on North Vietnam were initiated, for example, and then rapidly increased under the incorrect assumption that such action would prevent the North Vietnamese from supporting the Vietcong. History indicates that the exact opposite occurred.

Then, in 1965, a battalion of three thousand five hundred Marines arrived in country, marking the first significant number of combat troops to enter the fray. That event is generally regarded as the first point at which the United States became involved in the ground war. Just about the time the class of 1966 graduated, troop strength had swelled to over 385,000. A number of the Brown NROTC members would soon add to that total. Public opinion at home, which had been distinctly in favor of our intervention at first, rapidly eroded, especially after the Tet Offensive in late 1967. Even though this aggressive action, huge invasion, and push by the Vietcong and North Vietnamese regulars resulted in massive losses to them, it was still clear in the aftermath that our side was no closer to victory.

In 1968, when Richard Nixon moved into Pennsylvania Avenue, there were an astounding 536,000 troops in South Vietnam, which was the highest total ever. An enormously unpopular Lyndon Johnson had wisely chosen to go back to the ranch and not run again. Under Nixon, a "Vietnamization" program strategy was implemented. The success of that effort was premised on our effectively being able to strengthening the army of the Republic of Vietnam so that they could take over the defense of their own country. What a novel idea! Coincidentally, Nixon did immediately begin a troop drawdown, and by early 1970, some 250,000 had come home.

Eventually by 1972, less than 25,000 remained in country, and most had been redeployed to positions along the coast and interior instead of on the borders, in an attempt to avoid combat confrontations. This too little, too late tactical shift did prove successful, and the net effect was to reduce casualties. The Paris Peace accords, such as they were, were signed in January 1973, and provided for the suspension of all

US offensive operations in Vietnam. We had sixty days to withdraw all personnel. The fighting for us was over.

While no one can argue about the cessation of hostilities being a good thing, the peace accords virtually rendered our fifteen-year herculean effort as almost straightaway meaningless. South Vietnam was taken over by the North with hardly a whimper, and almost immediately became the very communist country we had sought to avoid. Over fifty-eight thousand courageous American service members lost their lives in that star-crossed fifteen-year debacle, to say nothing of the one quarter of a million who were wounded. Among those who perished were several from Brown University, including two of the very finest— USMC Captains Charlie Pigott and Jerry Zimmer.

CHAPTER 7

Look Left and Look Right

As Brown University opened for the 199th year in the fall of 1962, it boasted an undergraduate enrollment of just over 2,400 students. Included in this total was the freshman class of 1966, numbering 675. At our graduation ceremony four years later, in June 1966, 571 undergraduate degrees were conferred. Somehow, about 100 or so of the original entering freshmen failed to finish in four years, but several of those folks did eventually complete their degrees later on. As rigorous and difficult as it was to gain admission to Brown, the relatively small attrition number of only about fifteen percent is a fine testament to the administration. Once Brown took a chance and admitted you, they gave you plenty of rope to make it through. Other than for disciplinary reasons, almost no student was dismissed for academic reasons without a chance to return after taking some time off. It is also remarkable that the "four-year degree" was alive and well in those days. That timeframe has long since effectively disappeared among most hopeful college undergraduates.

The far-reaching reputation of the university ensured even in those days that the student mix would be drawn from all across the country, with a smattering of foreign students. "Diversity," per se, was not invented yet. While there was an extra-heavy proportion from the northeast, there were representatives from almost every state. It was about an even mix of students from public and private schools.

There were, of course, no athletic scholarships. A high school senior who had applied for, taken the exam, and been awarded an NROTC scholarship faced two entrance hurdles. He must first gain admission to the university, which was hardly a given at a place like Brown, and then he must find a slot within the local campus NROTC unit proper, which were limited in number. In fact, the Brown unit had just twenty-six openings. The program provided for an eventual commission as an ensign in the Navy, or an option could be selected after the sophomore year to become a second lieutenant in the Marine Corps upon graduation. Jerry Zimmer, Charlie Pigott, David Taylor, Billy Peters, Tom Drummond, Paul Ryan, Paul Kelly, and I were among those who signed commitments as midshipmen on September 17, 1962, and all eventually opted for the USMC.

As we wandered around the Brown campus with our freshman beanies pulled down over our ears during those first few days, we still didn't quite know what to make of the place. (It didn't take long, though, for us to realize how goofy we looked in those stupid hats and to lose them very quickly.) The first assembly for all incoming freshmen at Brown was a convocation at Sayles Hall, which was a large turn-of-the century Romanesque-style edifice in the middle of the main campus near the student union. It was not hard to be impressed as all 675 members of the incoming class filed into the building. The ancient wooden floors creaked and squeaked as the students funneled in, and there was just enough mustiness in the air to convey a sense that the place was really old. The walls on each side were festooned with oil portraits of university presidents dating back almost 200 years. You couldn't miss the imposing carved and inlaid woodwork. Seating was arranged in rows of old wooden folding chairs facing a raised dais at the front, which bore a close resemblance to a pulpit, giving the entire gathering an almost church-like aura.

The very first test facing our allegedly brilliant group of new students was to seek out and find their assigned seats, which we would continue to occupy at successive convocations over the ensuing four years. Seating was by alphabet, so the challenge should not have been that tough. Academic proficiency and practical, real-life matters, however, don't always necessarily coordinate. Nonetheless, after several minutes and not without a certain amount of bumping and shoving, these straight-A, 1200+ SAT scorers, high school valedictorians, etc. were finally able to sit down. I sat up toward the right front between John DeLuca and David Deutsch. Charlie Pigott was lost somewhere in the middle, and, of course, Jerry Zimmer was with Steve Zwarg, all the way in the back. A respectful reverence fell over the group as a stocky man in a dark suit with a narrow tie, thick glasses, and balding pate moved to the podium. Popular Barnaby C. Keeney was in his seventh year as president as he adjusted the microphone, opened his notes, and cleared his throat.

He looked out at the audience whose rapt attention he held, and began in a measured and steady tone. "I want to welcome you all as the class of 1966 to Brown University. Just being here means that you are special. I do not have to tell you how difficult it is to gain admission to Brown. There are thousands of very qualified young people whom we could not admit but who would love to be sitting in your place. I cannot emphasize enough the opportunity that awaits. We have some of the best qualified faculty anywhere who will challenge and excite you. I invite you to pursue your interests to the utmost. There is so much here for you."

"I am not telling you that the next four years are going to be easy, because that most assuredly will not be the case. You will have to pay attention, work hard, attend classes, and turn in assignments on time. If you choose not to meet these minimal expectations, and, unfortunately, experience has proven to us that some of you will not take this advice, you are certain to fall by the wayside. You will not pass through the Van Wickle gates in four years. We cannot tolerate those who will not help themselves. We know you all have the ability or you wouldn't be here. Now, I want you to look to your left and to your right."

The president paused as the men swiveled their necks in either direction. He continued, "Mark my words; in four years, one of the three of you will not be here. It is up to you to decide if that missing person is going to be you."

He stopped again to let that sink in. "I would like to make one final point that I feel is extremely important. For many of you, being here and away from home is a brand-new experience. You are on your own. There is no one around to push you. No one here at Brown is going to get you up and make sure you get to class. If you want to make it through Brown University, you must go to class. Most professors will not even take attendance, but they will know who shows up. There will be events that you are required to attend, such as regular convocations in this very room. You dare not miss them either. Go to class, I urge you. That is why you are here. Again, I welcome you to Brown, and wish each of you the very best of success. We will be seeing each other from time to time over the next four years. Now, check your class schedules, buy your books, and get your university careers off on a good note."

As President Keeney stepped away from the podium to polite applause, the assembled group rose in unison and moved toward the door at the rear of the building. Considering President Keeney's remarks I wondered, "Well, here I am. This is what I signed up for. I hope the missing man is not going to be me." In the back, Jerry was up and one of the first out the door. He would soon discover that the name Zimmer had definite advantages when it came to exiting convocations. As to

Keeney's warnings, it just simply never occurred to Zim that he might not make it. He had a drive and determination even then where failure was not an option. Charlie, on the other hand, was most concerned about this tummy. He was hungry, and lunch was overdue. He had already painted a big "X" over the guy sitting to his right. Enough said; the loser was certainly not going to be him.

CHAPTER 8

Wedgie, Squat, and Chicken Plucker

THE FALL SEMESTER IN SEPTEMBER 1962 was well underway, and the neophytes were doing their best to cope with the daily rigors of college life. While ominous world events simmered in the background that would eventually dominate our very existence, they seemed very far removed from Trigonometry 101. The impending societal revolution that would influence virtually everything we knew and believed had not yet begun to creep into our everyday lives. The Beatles had not even gotten their "act together yet," so to speak. They had finally left Hamburg, Germany, and just made their first recoding at Abbey Road Studios. We took little notice of them or the gathering storms on the horizon. We were preoccupied with such mundane issues as buying textbooks, hustling around campus to classrooms, gauging appropriate shared bathroom and shower etiquette, and navigating through a heterogeneous mass of confused young men and women all rushing in different directions. And, oh yes, your new weird roommate. You thought your kid brother at home was a pain in the butt. At least he didn't burn incense and murmur prayers in the dark until 2:00 a.m. Everyone had to deal with a new roommate, who been assigned by the university using a formula more closely guarded than the one used to make Coca Cola.

Even the best of matchups had a period of adjustment. A few were terrific, most were tolerable, and several were disastrous.

Before very long, though, most of us figured out what it took to survive on a university campus where Mom did not have dinner ready at 6:00 p.m. We settled into a routine of waking up in just enough time to rush to our first class, hitting Ma Feeney's Refectory for lunch, and dashing back to our dorm room for a short regroup (i.e., nap) before trudging off to afternoon classes. Dinner was usually still around 6:00 p.m. or so. It was then time to hit the books in our rooms or perhaps the carrels at the Rock. Few rooms were dark much before midnight. No doubt, Barnaby Keeney's advice had struck the fear in many of us who were appropriately intimidated, at least at first.

It went without saying, however, that the wisdom of his words did not penetrate the crania of the entire freshman class. We had several blithe spirits who were sure that they could get by on wit and guile alone. Class attendance and cracking books were decidedly infrequent activities. In fairly short order, most of that group were plying their academic indifferences elsewhere, at state Us, I suppose. Surprisingly, though, even at Brown, some of these folks not only skimped along, but actually did quite well.

Jerry, Charlie, and I were definitely not in that group. We worked hard and earned every passing grade we received. Perhaps it was because we knew that a boatswain's chair and paint chipping chisel on the USS *Enterprise* was a realistic alternative.

Back at the ancient, classic, but decidedly shabby Littlefield Hall, I was gradually adapting to communal living with minimal sound insulation. My roommate from Indiana, Doug Ogden, was also in the NROTC program, which I suppose cinched our match at University Hall. In fact, Doug eventually left Brown when he received an appointment to the Naval Academy, which I believe had been his first choice anyway. We got along pretty well.

Looking back now, perhaps I have been a little hasty to indict Brown's roommate and dorm assignment procedures. Littlefield was old and showed the effects of years of hard-living students. In our class, several other football players also had been placed in Littlefield. Someone had apparently figured out that the gridiron guys tended to be a bit rougher on living facilities than were the musicians. Littlefield could handle them. The sound of free weights being smashed against the concrete floor could be heard well into the night. Hall hockey, of course, was a mandatory sport for every new student in those days. Shaving cream fights were continual, and water balloons rained down from the upper floors on a regular basis. A young man with a good arm and just the right trajectory could manage to heave them out of a window where they could explode on unsuspecting cars moving along George Street. The campus cops made many calls to Littlefield. Most times they would arrive to discover all students fast asleep in their beds or cramming diligently for their next exam. Disturbance? What disturbance? Must have been those fraternity jerks across the street.

Beer, of course, was then, as it is now, the great social lubricant. The Rhode Island minimum drinking age of 21 and prohibition against having alcoholic beverages within the dorm rooms made little difference to most students. Either Schlitz Haus or Narragansett Hogan might have been more appropriate names for our dorm. Poor Larry Gross, the upper class proctor, who lived on the first floor, accepted most of the grief for the pranks and unruly conduct of his charges. At first he came on as a by-the-book martinet but soon revealed himself as a nice guy who would keep his door shut until the hall water began to seep into his room or when he noticed the EMS lights flashing out in the street. Nearby, Charlie and Jerry experienced dorm life very much the same.

A word needs to be said at this point about nicknames, which at the same time can be fascinating and confounding. Nicknames are a phenomenon that always seems to emerge as groups of kids become very good friends, or perhaps when those who feel uncomfortable begin to interact. Rarely, if ever, does anyone have a personal choice in the selection of his or her alternate moniker. They are doled out indiscriminately without request. Some stick, others vanish. I have no idea why. Perhaps college students are too lazy to take the time to learn given names, but the nicknames that seem to take are handed out almost as badges of honor. Someone yells out something and somehow magically it fits. Very often, the origins of new identifiers become lost as quickly as they appear. Littlefield Hall in 1962-63, for instance, was inhabited by the Sow, Thunder, Boomer, Wedgie, Squat, Chicken Plucker, Tool, King Rooster, and several others.

It is perhaps not necessary to say that you were much more likely to be a candidate for a nickname if you happened to be an active prankster. Reserved and serious, studious residents tended to be exempt. Once a nickname caught on, you were stuck. Love it or hate it, there was no denying or avoiding. You only prayed some dumb student did not address you as such while your mother was around for parents' weekend.

Of course, there are exceptions to every rule and as memory serves, for reasons that are long since forgotten, neither Charlie nor Jerry were forced to bear the weight of an assigned nickname. Perhaps it was the force of Charlie's assertive personality that enabled him to avoid such a stigma, or perhaps his nickname has just been lost over time. The closest he came was a very unremarkable "Chas." Jerry had the benefit of having a built-in, easy to remember nickname. Zimmer easily morphed to "Zim," and you were done. I, however, was not so fortunate, and over the course of my time at Brown bore the brunt of several aliases. In the dorm I became known as "Squat," which must have been associated with my rugged stature that featured width rather than height. Also, for reasons that are certainly buried forever, Charlie Pigott would always refer to me as "Eight Ball." The good news is that that one did not spread.

CHAPTER 9

Join the Navy-That Sounds Cool

AT THE START OF THE tumultuous 1960s, some half-century ago, the cost of a Brown University education, even then, was for most families, prohibitively high. In 1960, gas was $.31 per gallon. We had the $.04 postage stamp for a letter, which was how almost all personal communications were transmitted. Movies were a buck, and you could purchase a beautiful new home for $15,000. The $2,000 to $3,000 Brown tuition before books, board, and beer was indeed a princely sum in those days.

Also, as has been touched on above, attitudes toward serving in our nation's military were far different than they would become in the decades that followed after Vietnam malaise seeped into the fabric of our society. In fact, when as high school seniors we were formally applying to college, appointments to Annapolis and West Point were every bit as revered, perhaps even more than admission to an Ivy League university. The military as a career, if not for everyone, was generally regarded as a noble and highly respected profession.

In the fall of 1961 when I was just starting my senior year in high school, my mother came across an article in the *Boston Globe* entitled "How would you like to send your son to Harvard for free?" It caught her attention. The writer discussed the United States Navy's Holloway Plan, which had been created by a little-known law passed in 1946. Some fifty-one universities participated in the program across the country. The plan was designed to create a source of officers for the Navy from those individuals who did not attend the US Naval Academy at Annapolis. Each year, some twenty to twenty-five thousand high school seniors took a rigorous competitive exam for two thousand places allocated in NROTC units at the participating universities.

The Navy paid full tuition, books, fees, and provided a stipend of $50.00 per month. Upon graduation, each person would receive a regular commission in the United States Navy or Marine Corps. They would be obligated to serve at least one year for each year of college. This program at that time was unique to the Navy and enabled many very bright students the means to get through Brown and other very expensive universities. It was a terrific arrangement that seemed to be a win-win for all parties involved, especially the university. Charlie, Jerry, and I were among the full scholarship recipients that made up the midshipmen class of 1966. We were hardly poor, but my father was employed by the federal government and worked very hard for every dollar he earned. With a brother and two sisters behind me, it was very doubtful that I could have afforded to attend Brown without the NROTC scholarship.

A distinction should be made that this discussion has been about the "regular" NROTC program. There was also a "contract" program, where a student could sign up without any competitive exam. He would basically follow the same path as regular midshipmen, except that there was no scholarship involved. There were several contract midshipmen in the Brown unit who would receive "reserve" commissions upon graduation. It is regrettable that, following the wave of rage of all things military, this program was summarily exorcised from Brown in the early 1970s. More will be discussed about that situation later.

At first blush, it might have appeared somewhat telling that the Department of Naval Science was relegated to a building that had been completed in 1891. On the other hand, Lyman Hall was centrally located, and had been originally built as a gymnasium. There was ample open area to permit formations and limited close order drill. There was even an elevated running track. When the new Marvel Gymnasium opened, most all gym-related activities were shifted to that location. The Lyman Hall gym was restricted to boxing and a few other activities. In 1946, NROTC took occupancy and remained there until the entire program was dropped by Brown in 1972. The building has since been re-adapted for theater arts. The Brown NROTC unit had been established as one of initial eighteen country wide in 1940 in response to the desperate need for officers in World War II. That Brown played a key role from this perspective in that conflict seems to have been long forgotten or ignored.

Although the years have blurred somewhat the personalities and credentials of many of the staff instructors in the Department of Naval Science in the early 1960s, just as the Vietnam War was gathering steam, there were three particular men who were to exert great influence on Jerry, Charlie, and me. The titular Professor of Naval Science was Captain Brent, who was supported by his executive officer, Commander Walsh. Both were career Navy officers. While these gentlemen were accomplished professionals in their own right, the men who really mattered to us were then Major Charles Webster, Staff Sergeant Ronald R. Benoit, and Major Richard Whelan, all USMC. Based upon the program parameters, all midshipmen followed the same track until their junior (i.e., second class) year. At that point, it was possible to select a Marine Corps option in lieu of ultimate service in the Navy. The Marines on staff had everything to do with who took that option, which ended up being eight of our total class, including Paul Kelly, Paul Ryan,

Tom Drummond, Billy Peters, David Taylor, Charlie, Jerry, and me. The inspirational and extraordinary personalities of those three staff jarheads had absolutely everything to do with all of us opting for the Corps.

As an NROTC midshipman at Brown, you essentially enjoyed the same freedom as any other non-ROTC student, but there were certain additional specific obligations that had to be met. For one, you were required to enroll in one Naval Science course each semester. Yes, subjects like military history and seamanship were included, and full credit for graduation was given for these courses, which were taught by Naval and Marine officers on staff at the NROTC unit. You also had to take and pass university physics and calculus courses, which would be no mean feat for some, including me. Weekly, you had to attend two hours of drill in full uniform. Frequently these sessions were held indoors, but often we literally marched around campus, to the mounting ridicule of some students as the years passed.

Each summer, you were obligated to make a "cruise" for six weeks or so out with the real US Navy. The first year, you were assigned to a ship and functioned as enlisted man. The second year, everyone spent three weeks at the Naval Air Station in Corpus Christi, Texas, for flight training orientation and then three weeks in Little Creek, Virginia, doing amphibious landings. Finally, if you remained on a Navy track, between your junior and senior years, you went back aboard ship as an "almost" junior officer. The Marine options were sent to Quantico, Virginia, for Officers' Candidate School training.

There has always been a wide variety of opinion about the applicability of this program to a university campus, and to Brown in particular. As three who had matriculated through the program, Charlie, Jerry, and I, to a man, steadfastly agreed that NROTC definitely belonged on the Brown campus. It would be disingenuous to assert that the NROTC courses were among the more rigorous within the overall curriculum, but they were certainly no easier than dozens of other courses given by the university proper. They were hardly "gut" courses. In fact, in order to receive a Brown degree, midshipmen had to take one extra university course, which was not required of other students.

The summer cruises were fun, and generally took us to interesting places. The cruises were always shared by NROTC students from other universities, including Harvard, Yale, Cornell, Villanova, Auburn, Florida, and many more. The bottom line, of course, was that it was very gratifying to walk through the registrar's line at the start of each semester and see your tuition charge on your invoice already stamped "PAID." No student loans to dog you forever after graduation. And then there was that beautiful blue monthly check for $50.00 that magically showed up in your mailbox every month. That was big money to a kid in the 1960s. We always had plenty of beer money—and most of the other students knew it.

As the Vietnam War dragged on, discontent with the administration in Washington and the military became widespread, with a mini-epicenter erupting on the Brown campus. To a degree, this situation is fully understandable. The imposition of the draft presented a very personal and direct threat to virtually all students. No one, it seemed, wanted to serve in such an unpopular war. The Brown faculty, who were always resentful of the Department of Naval Science with a full professorship status and a lightly regarded curricula regimen, fanned the flames and pushed to remove ROTC from the campus.

In November 1967, the student government passed a resolution that ROTC was not compatible with Brown. The local chapter of the American Association of University Professors concurred. In 1969, the faculty voted 155 to 55 to end all certified ROTC programs at Brown. By 1972, all the programs were gone. With the expulsion went some one hundred full scholarships, to say nothing of waiting job opportunities for graduates. There is an irony here that such a liberal place, where almost anything goes and the right to express your own free opinions is sublime, one particular avenue of endeavor, which is personally abhorrent to some, was summarily barred from an otherwise sky-is-the-limit venue. Free love was just fine, but serving your country was somehow reprehensible.

CHAPTER 10

Charlie and the Rat Factory

IT IS POPULAR TODAY TO be very critical of college football. Head injuries, sexual abuse, bullying, taking monetary advantage of players, and sundry other issues keep the talking heads buzzing 24/7. In many cases, such fault finding, especially when it comes to overemphasis, is absolutely justified. The sport has always had its detractors. Even at a pigskin backwater like Brown in the early 1960s, when three wins was a "good" season, there were zero athletic scholarships, and no post-season involvement, there were still rumblings that the game had no place on the campus. (Is there an echo in here?) Such grander issues aside, even after I realized my playing days were numbered, I still did remain on the freshman squad for the entire season. I have no regrets about having done that. The guys I met, with the unspoken bonds that emerged on that dusty field in mid-September, became some of my closest friends at Brown. Charlie Pigott and Jerry Zimmer were prominently included among them.

Hanging in there when my playing chances were remote also yielded other benefits. It took me a while to recognize it, but, strangely enough, putting all those hours on the practice field paid dividends in the classroom. Normally during the season we didn't get through "knocking heads" until well after 6:30 p.m. every evening, which forced us to shower and hustle back to the refectory where Ma Feeney held our suppers late. Typically, it was around 9:00 p.m. before I was able to finally sit down in my dorm room and think about hitting the books. Without football, I could have been there for at least two to three hours earlier, to say nothing about being bone weary from practice.

It was only in my sophomore year, when I had given up the sport and my grades were trending downward that I realized; that tight and demanding football schedule actually forced me to study more. I had to budget the short allotted time. When I had the luxury of extra hours of "free" time they somehow got eaten up with other things. My grades, which were never poor, were always better when I was playing a sport than otherwise. But I was certainly never tempted to put on a helmet again. Isn't it an established fact that football players are superior in the classroom to their non-playing contemporaries?

Charlie Pigott was truly a very good football player, but like many of us, he'd had just enough of it by the time our second year rolled around. He decided not to play again either. A Brown varsity football game program from November 1962 has a page devoted to our freshman team. There is a photo of the entire squad. Appropriately, I am way in the back row, Jerry is in the middle, and Charlie is right up front. The underlying article is titled "The Record Belies the True Picture." I think we ended three up and three down. Charlie is identified in the piece as one of the "boys who has risen to the surface." I guess the coach's comments about Jerry and I must have been edited out for column space reasons?

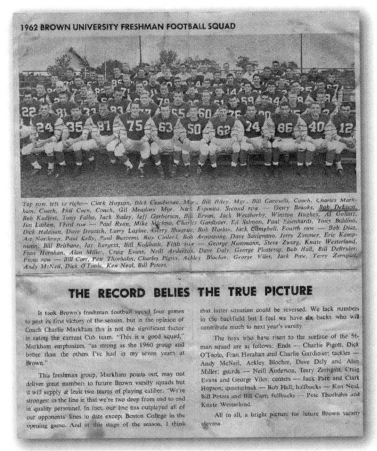

1962 BROWN UNIVERSITY FRESHMAN FOOTBALL SQUAD

Top row, left to right— Clark Hopson, Dick Casabonne, Mgr., Bill Riley, Mgr., Bill Caroselli, Coach, Charles Markham, Coach, Phil Coen, Coach, Gil Meadors Mgr. Nick Esposito. Second row — Gary Brooks, Bob DeLuca, Bob Kudless, Tony Falbo, Jack Staley, Jeff Garberson, Bill Ervan, Jack Weatherby, Winston Hughes, Al Gollatz, Jim Larkin. Third row — Paul Ryan, Mike Machno, Charles Gardiner, Ed Salmon, Paul Eisenhardt, Tony Baldino, Dick Halajian, Dave Deutsch, Larry Lapine, Gerry Shugrue, Bob Harlan, Jack Campbell. Fourth row — Bob Diaz, Art Northrup, Paul Kelly, Paul Buscemi, Roy Cioleri, Bob Armstrong, Dave Savignano, Jerry Zimmer, Eric Kampmann, Bill Brahane, Jay Burgess, Bill Kolibah. Fifth row — George Hunemann, Steve Zwarg, Knute Westerlund, Fran Horahan, Alan Miller, Craig Evans, Neill Anderson, Dave Daly, Dave Plasteras, Bob Hall, Bill DeBruler, Front row — Bill Carr, Pete Thorbahn, Charles Pigott, Ackley Blocher, George Viles, Jack Pate, Terry Zerngast, Andy McNeil, Dick O'Toole, Ken Neal, Bill Peters.

THE RECORD BELIES THE TRUE PICTURE

It took Brown's freshman football squad four games to post its first victory of the season, but in the opinion of Coach Charlie Markham this is not the significant factor in rating the current Cub team. "This is a good squad," Markham emphasizes, "as strong as the 1960 group and better than the others I've had in my seven years at Brown."

This freshman group, Markham points out, may not deliver great numbers to future Brown varsity squads but it will supply at least two teams of playing caliber. "We're stronger in the line in that we're two deep from end to end in quality personnel. In fact, our line has outplayed all of our opponents' lines to date except Boston College in the opening game. And at this stage of the season, I think

that latter situation could be reversed. We lack numbers in the backfield but I feel we have six backs who will contribute much to next year's varsity.

The boys who have risen to the surface of the 56-man squad are as follows: Ends — Charlie Pigott, Dick O'Toole, Fran Horahan and Charlie Gardiner; tackles — Andy McNeil, Ackley Blocher, Dave Daly and Alan Miller; guards — Neill Anderson, Terry Zerngast, Craig Evans and George Viles; centers — Jack Pate and Clark Hopson; quarterback — Bob Hall; halfbacks — Ken Neal, Bill Peters and Bill Carr; fullbacks — Pete Thorbahn and Knute Westerlund.

All in all, a bright picture for future Brown varsity elevens.

The Brown University freshman football team. Charlie Pigott (Front Row, No. 87) was identified as as one of the players who had "risen to the surface". Jerry Zimmer (Third Row, No.51) and Bob DeLuca (Last Row, Upper Left, No.55) did not receive such notoriety.

Any coach will tell you that it is up to team members to make contributions in whatever way possible. As it turned out during that otherwise unspectacular freshman year, I was able to play a very important role in one of those victories. You must indeed know your role on a team. Other than as cannon fodder in scrimmages to build up the confidence of the starting players, my role on the Brown freshman team as a player was virtually non-existent. You never know, however, when fate my step in and open an unexpected door.

The Yale game that year gave me such an opportunity. As everyone knows, New England weather is very fickle, especially in the fall. In the space of a few weeks, we could go from practicing in the sweltering ninety-degree heat of September to the biting chill of early November. It was late in the season, when the Yale Bull Pups (i.e., freshman team) came to Providence. Unfortunately, they chose a day when the weather turned for the worse. In fact, it was one of those dark and blustery afternoons when "it sure looks like snow." Well, as a matter of fact, it did snow that day—a whole lot. In fact, by the end of the game, the entire field was covered, and the yard line markings were totally obscured. Normally, I really liked the snow. As kids growing up in Massachusetts, we often played tackle football in the snow. It cushioned the impact of hitting, and you really couldn't get moving too fast.

On that day at Brown, our team apparently felt the same way. We played a very competitive game, and in fact, won the contest in the fourth quarter, when one of our defensive tackles ripped the ball away from a Yale halfback and lumbered home for the game's only score. In referring to the team as "we" above, I do imply that I was a part thereof. Well, perhaps not quite that day from a traditional competitive player's perspective, since I guess I was sworn by implication to impartiality.

The inclement weather made travel difficult, and the game officials found they were short a person to man the first down marker chains. Most of the other scrubs on the sideline, Jerry Zimmer included, sensed impending trouble, and melted into the mass of players. I was left standing there alone deep into my own thoughts with snowflakes building up on my faceguard. Suddenly, Coach Markham screamed out my name. I was taken aback that he even knew it.

Coaching is, of course, a balancing act. Proper personnel decisions are key to victory. Despite the fact that he would be greatly reducing his team's depth off the bench, he unselfishly sacrificed me to fill the chain gang vacancy. He persisted despite my objections that the bad weather would very likely force him to use his sixth and seventh stringers in the game. Very reluctantly I shuffled over and joined the chain gang. For the entire game, in full uniform, including my helmet, I held the "dumb" end of the chain. I suppose my predicament was roughly akin to Josh Groban selling popcorn at Carnegie Hall. At least I could say that I accomplished something that day that I hadn't otherwise been able to do. I got on the field during a game, if only for close first down measurements. It would not have been nearly so humiliating had I not been in uniform and been able to remain relatively anonymous.

Of course, the razz talk immediately started the next day as I sat down in Naval Science 101 class next to Jerry, who immediately inquired about my blisters or frostbite from having to hold that cold metal pole. For several weeks thereafter as I walked around campus, many of my buddies had a great time reminding me that they'd seen ferocious "Number 55" holding that pole in the snow. I think there was even an Admiral Perry reference or two. On the other hand, I suppose for the first time since high school, I had finally measured up on the football field.

I was hardly thinking much about football when we returned to campus from semester break in late January 1963. I decided to try my luck at lacrosse, a game that I had never played but looked interesting. In order to prepare his teams for the season that began in March the lacrosse coach, Cliff Stevenson, liked to practice on the asphalt parking lots at Aldrich-Dexter Field after having the snow pushed off. It is a wonder that I was not recruited for that job. I ended up playing the sport three years with very moderate success. Again, I was essentially anonymous to the coach, who never spoke my name until somehow I scored two goals against the University of Connecticut. I did enjoy playing the game and admired guys like Jerry Zimmer, who were very good at it.

In those days, high school lacrosse was limited nationally to a few hotbed areas, particularly around Baltimore and upstate New York, including where Jerry was from in the Binghamton area. Lacrosse is a running game that also requires a fair amount of body contact. Jerry had played in high school, and while his smallish but rugged stature was not quite right for football, he was perfect for lacrosse. He could run all day and played midfield with grace and speed. He and Billy Peters, who also would go on to be a Marine, often played on the same line. They combined for several goals, including a key one against Tufts our freshman year.

The Brown Univeristy freshman lacrosse team. Thanks to Jerry Zimmer (No.18) who was already an excellent player, Bob DeLuca (No. 30) decided to give it a try but somehow never lived up to Jerry's promise that he'd be soon running and cradling the ball with his stick like an Iriquois warrior.

We all loved sports, but life as a student at Brown certainly offered much, much more. Studying and partying were at the top of the list, although maybe not in that order. Despite the Navy bucks, some of us had to work to make ends meet. There were all kinds of student jobs to be had in places like the Rock and the refectory ("Rat-Factory"). Speaking of eating, it is hard to fathom today, but Brown actually had a requirement that we all had to dress for dinner. We actually were supposed to wear a jacket and tie for the evening meal. Fortunately, that ridiculous rule disappeared early on while we were there.

The dining hall was arranged such that the food prep and serving area was in the central core of a very large room that was filled with wooden tables and chairs. On the perimeter of this room there were individual dining rooms for certain organizations, principally the fraternities. Privacy was afforded each of these rooms by swinging doors.

It must have been sometime in the spring one evening in the middle of the week. I had just finished my meal with a group of Littlefield buddies. We were sitting out in the open area at a table not far from the door to the Pi Lambda Phi dining room. To get your food it was necessary for students to form lines outside the central serving area. You would grab a tray and walk inside where there were counters and steam tables. You would push your tray along on a sliding surface made up of metal rails. Each student would make his selection known to someone behind the counter, who would then dish it out. At the end of the line, you took your loaded tray and went back out to find a table to sit and eat. Desserts were generally laid out in groups on individual plates that you grabbed yourself as you moved through the line. In most cases, even the fraternity guys had to do the same thing.

Just as I was considering getting a refill on my milk that evening, the Pi Lam dining room door flew open and a tall, thin, bespectacled brother (fraternity brother) emerged wearing his mandated sport coat, button-down shirt, and dreary green weenie tie. The gentleman was clearly not happy. In fact, he was pissed. His face, which was otherwise pallid from many, many hours in the carrels at the Rock, was laced with red as he struggled to control his anger. He clutched in his hands one of Ma Feeney's favorite desserts: a square of tasty cake drizzled with delicious strawberry topping. He aimed straight for the serving line and disappeared inside.

I just couldn't pass that one up and barely beat the crowd that rushed to see just what this guy's problem was. Once I got inside, I saw the man, with feet apart, glaring and pointing at one of the student servers behind the dessert section. "Who is responsible for this outrage?" demanded the frat guy in a high-pitched voice that cracked with emotion. There was no immediate response, so he tried again. "Was it you, asshole?"

Now the gentleman had gotten personal, which was just too much for a proud Marine-to-be to take. The man calmly made a slight adjustment to his white server's coat. Daggers bounced back at the interloper as he looked up. Charlie Pigott fired back, "What's the matter, Dweeb? Don't you like sponge cake? No one else has complained." Try as he might, Charlie found it impossible to be angry. He could hardly hide the smirk on his face.

Charlie had decided to supplement one of Ma's dessert offerings with a slightly heartier ingredient. He had sliced up one of the sponges they used to wipe down the tables into a square which was the same size as the real cake and then copiously covered it with the red strawberry goo. The lucky recipient of his treat had obviously been more than a little surprised as he tried to eat his dessert. Charlie was quick to point out later that he had been very careful to use only a brand-new sponge and not a used one. He claimed to have been ever mindful of the man's digestive tract.

Despite his ire, it is unlikely that the unfortunate frat guy would have pressed the issue further, once he took measure of his rugged, hulking adversary. It is also doubtful if Charlie would have taken him on anyway. After all, it was just a harmless joke. In any event, we will never know, because all of a sudden Ma Feeney herself burst on the scene. Marshal Dillon finally gets to the Long Branch. In fact, Charlie might not have even lost his job over the whole thing if he had only kept his mouth shut. It was just too much when in the presence of the big boss, he inquired of the guy from Phi Lam, "We don't waste food here in the refectory. You know, the kids in Biafra and all. If you will finish up that portion and give me just a minute, I will get you some seconds."

The dweeb was livid. Ma Feeney was not amused. Charlie had to hit the bricks. The rest of us were ecstatic.

CHAPTER 11

Two Pilots Are Born

SPRING WAS IN THE AIR and musings of the summer break were beginning to creep into those long, cloistered study sessions, especially when the weather was so agreeable outside. Beatlemania had erupted in the United Kingdom with over a million "I Want to Hold Your Hand" records sold. The US was listening but not quite convinced as yet. The second semester had only a few more weeks to run when one day, Lieutenant Evans, the freshman Naval Science instructor, "passed the word" that there would be a field trip coming up. It is significant to note that every branch of the military has its own set of proprietary terms and expressions that border on being a language unto itself. The Navy's left = port, right = starboard, etc. You get the picture. You don't "announce"; you pass the word. Charlie Pigott especially reveled in mimicking Navy talk.

On April 20th, the entire group of about thirty fourth class midshipmen would board a plane at the Quonset Point Naval Air Station in southern Rhode Island and fly to the air training facility at Pensacola, Florida. The purpose of the trip was to give us young men an orientation into naval aviation. Even then, when the Vietnam conflict was barely heating up, there was already a push for pilots. For years to come, the glorification of streaking through the skies was a constant theme wherever you were exposed to NROTC propaganda.

*For most, our first plane ride in early 1963 ever, as midshipmen
fourth class from Quonset Point, Rhode Island to Pensacola,
Florida. The Navy was pitching hard for pilots, and it worked.*

It was a seasonally chilly but clear morning as the group assembled
on the sidewalk in front of Lyman Hall to board a bus for Quonset
Point. If nothing else, it would be warmer in Florida. We young naval
candidates were decked in our full khaki summer service Alpha uniforms. This occasion marked one of the first times we sort of had it all
together from a uniform standpoint. We were supposed to be imperson-
ating young naval officers. Well, in fact, Halloween was a few months
past, and a few of our crew would have fit in well for that occasion. Most
wore their new outfits passably well, but there is always that 10 percent
that never seem to catch on. It is an unwritten military regulation that
any assembled group must mill aimlessly around for a minimum of at

least ten minutes before any special reason for their gathering becomes apparent. Much, much longer waits are quite commonplace.

As the crowd stood waiting for the show to literally get on the road, I turned to fellow Midshipman Jeff Hayes and glared incredulously at his neck. "What the heck is that thing?" I demanded in a shrill tone and voice level that I knew was sure to catch the attention of others nearby. "Is that some kind of weapon or birth control device? Do you expect to get lucky in Florida?" I wagged my finger at a small gray wire with a pointed sharp end that was somehow configured with a coiled spring. The contraption was sticking out from under Midshipman Hayes' starched collar.

Jeff glanced down and immediately realized his bewildering "spiffy" had popped loose on one side. A spiffy was a collar stay device that would prove to be at least 90 percent unreliable for the intended purpose, but was nonetheless a required part of the naval uniform. The damned thing was supposed to hold down otherwise floppy dress shirt collars. No button-downs allowed. It just never seemed to stay hidden and was a bugger to put on. It must be remembered that this was long before Internet "customer reviews" came into vogue. Otherwise, the contraption's sales would have peaked at a dozen or two.

Jeff, a *bon vivant* at heart, who went on to become my close friend, roommate, and fraternity brother, was never one to miss an opportunity to react in kind. He reached up and ripped the offending implement from around his neck, somehow avoiding drawing blood. He flipped it over the head of a couple of rows of his colleagues, where it just missed the approaching Lieutenant Commander Hall, who was about to pass the word about the events of the trip.

Jeff contritely allowed, "Midshipman DeLuca, I would have stuck that point in your fat butt, except that you'd never have felt it through these monkey suits they are making us wear." The field trip was off to an inspiring start.

As an unabashed pilot recruiting promo, the weekend was certainly a success. The flight orientation at NAS, Pensacola, was definitely interesting, if not especially challenging. It consisted of attending lectures, watching a few USN-produced promo films, and being able to walk up, look at, and touch some real airplanes in their hangars. The event was topped off by a chance to enjoy some real Navy mess chow for the first time. Each man was photographed in a flight suit with a picture of an F9 Cougar two-seat jet fighter in the background. These pictures became each man's "official" Navy aviation photograph. In fact, several made their way to hometown newspapers, even though the guys involved never actually followed through with naval aviation. In a few cases, though, as in the cases of Charlie, Jerry, Chip Horahan, Billy Peters, Dave Taylor, and some others, these snapshots were true harbingers of the future.

Basic rah-rah Navy aviation aside, this trip was marked by a couple of noteworthy events. For me, personally, and very likely for most of the group then in early 1963, the flight from Rhode Island to Florida in that Navy Convair two-engine prop transporter was our very first flight in an airplane. That in itself was really quite a thrill. Most of us, who prided ourselves on maintaining an air of sophistication and worldliness, revealed a bit of the gregarious kids that we really were. We remained transfixed to the window ports for much of the trip. "Look-at those ants down there. And the toy cars!" The weather was clear and the visibility excellent, which also made for a smooth ride. There were no "stews" with rolling trollies of food on board, but even the Navy-supplied box lunches were well received. Times were much different fifty-plus years ago. It was still possible to impress a teenager.

Besides the first flight kick, the other item of note occurred just before the group was about to leave Pensacola. The Brown midshipmen were told to assemble in front of the administration building at 1500 hours sharp to board a bus that would take us back to the plane for the return flight to Rhode Island. As was the drill, the group "fell in" as instructed at the appointed time. Mandatory milling and waiting ensued. Finally a head count was taken, and somehow the number was two midshipmen short. Otherwise, the group was ready to go. The plane was waiting. Once they were assured that the most likely suspect, Jeff Hayes, was dutifully present, some consternation set in as to who was missing. It turned out that Charlie and Jerry had not made it back from the mess hall to the formation. Maybe they hadn't yet figured out how to calculate military time? (I mean, 1500 is five o'clock. Right?) Someone in the crowd remembered overhearing Charlie say something about looking at the jets again. Sure enough, the two missing men were discovered out on the tarmac next to an F4B Phantom. The duo was listening intently to a real Navy pilot whom they had run across and were enraptured by all the guy had to offer. They had completely lost track of the time. Two Marine pilots may have been born that day.

CHAPTER 12
The USS Wasp

WITH THE ARDUOUS FRESHMAN YEAR finally in the books, most students got to return home to relax on the beach, pursue soft summer jobs, or just sleep in for a while. Everyone was relieved when the second semester final exams were finally over. Ultimate relief, however, was dependent upon the trickling back with passing grades on those little postcards we'd left with each professor after taking his exam. Once that happened, everything was really cool. It was time to put Brown U in the rearview mirror for a couple of months.

Not so fast, NROTC chaps; your freshman cruise was literally on deck. And you were under orders for the first time. Your unwinding would be delayed a while until late July and August. What's the matter? Didn't you read the fine print? You now served at the convenience of the Chief of Naval Operations. It was time to find out about the real seagoing Navy. Ahoy, lads!

With the nation's security squarely on the line, the CNO decided it would be in the best interests of our common defense to have Charlie, Jerry, myself, and a couple of dozen other NROTC students report punctually on June 2, 1963, to the USS *Wasp* at the Navy wharf in Boston. For me, getting there was pretty easy, since I lived in Framingham, which was only about 20 miles away.

On the designated morning my mother drove me in, and I kissed her good-bye on the dock. It was hardly a Lauren Bacall-Humphrey Bogart departure as I executed a smart about face and marched up the gangway, being careful to salute both the US flag and the officer of the deck, which I had learned in Naval Science 101. Once on board, I dutifully made my presence known and was immediately ordered to do nothing until 0800 the next morning. Those were the days long before cell phones, and after giving my mother enough time to drive home, I found a pay phone and asked her to come back and pick me up. I got to spend one more night in my own bed. Hey, I was just a kid.

The next morning my sweet mother, after making her third trip into Boston, was left standing there on the pier as the huge ship actually cast off with me on board. She had lived through World War II, and our departure brought back her memories of several similar scenes with my father, who served in the Coast Guard. At that time things were far different. Everyone quietly understood that some of the men would not be coming back. Many of the good-byes were indeed final. Normally very stoic, she told me later that she found herself choked up as the *Wasp* glided away. I do not think future generations will ever appreciate what those folks went through.

Although I wasn't so sure at first, I think our group drew a long straw by getting dispatched to that huge floating hunk of steel that passed for an aircraft carrier. The aging *Wasp* was sort of the Littlefield Hall of boats. A few of the guys were assigned to relatively tiny "tin cans" (i.e., destroyers) that would accompany us. The USS *Wasp* was launched in November 1943, which made it almost 20, and a year older than most of us. It was 876 feet long and carried eighty to one hundred airplanes, including many helicopters. Supposedly its boiler-driven propulsion system with four propellers could move the monster up to thirty-three knots. It had an angled deck configuration, which meant air operations with launching and recovering aircraft could in theory happen at the same time. There were two catapults and four arrestor landing cables. Fully staffed it carried three thousand five hundred enlisted men, one hundred fifteen officers, and a few dozen confused college kids. Designated "CVS-18," the *Wasp* was a support carrier with the primary mission of anti-submarine warfare. There was a lot to see and plenty for us to get into.

The mighty USS WASP where we served defending our shores during the summer of 1963. It was tough duty, but someone had to do it. We only put in at world hot spots in New Orleans, St. Thomas, Puerto Cortes, Honduras, and Jamaica.

Oh, and there was the other factor: our itinerary. We were in for some rough ports of call. They were really asking a lot of us college students who had just had to endure nine months of beer drinking, partying, and grab-ass with a little schoolwork thrown in now and then. The ship moved out into the Atlantic and steamed due south around Florida into the Gulf of Mexico, where we tied up at New Orleans for a week. We then spent another week floating around the Caribbean, with the next stop at Puerto Cortes, Honduras. After only a two-day stay there, we spent the Fourth of July on the Island of Jamaica. I guess the Navy was feeling bad for us at that point, so they decided to let up just a bit and our last stop was St. Thomas in the Virgin Islands.

We arrived back in Boston on the 24th of July, about seven weeks from when we had started. Talk about the Love Boat! I am not sure how anyone could have devised a better trip for a group of college boys who were looking to chill out from a long year in school. Our compliments to the tour director.

Before I give the impression that this collective sea duty assignment was just one big, long party, please be assured that we were duly sworn midshipman third class, who formed an integral part of the superior fighting machine that was the USS *Wasp*. We had duties, responsibilities, and labored tirelessly to be assured our shores were well defended. Despite our good intentions, however, the Navy system somehow did not fully provide for us middies on active duty aboard seagoing vessels. We sort of looked like sailors with the blue dungaree trousers, light-blue chambray shirts, and Dixie cup hats with a dark-blue band around the top. We wore no insignia of any other kind. The enlisted men just weren't sure who or what we were supposed to be—officers or men. So, they ignored us for the most part. The officers knew we weren't officers, and didn't have a whole lot to do with us either. It was a huge ship, and with no one really worried about us there was plenty of room to hide out and pick and choose what we wanted to do. Most of us were able to avoid swabbing the deck or that dreaded throwing the trash and garbage over the fantail detail.

A Navy ship in those days was organized into several departments and divisions, according to function. There were, for instance, the Deck, Navigation, Operations, and Engineering Departments, among many others. We were told that while on the *Wasp* we would rotate through several divisions to get an idea how they functioned. We would be closely supervised by outstanding professionals and also get a chance to try our hand at actual work assignments in the departments. All that certainly sounded logical, but it didn't take long for us clever college kids to figure out that nobody was really watching us. Did you really want to spend time down in the Engineering Division way below decks in the engine room? Typically, it was over 100 degrees down there and you couldn't hear yourself think.

Once we found an area of the ship that was interesting and relatively pleasant, we tended to hang out there for as long as we wanted. For me that turned out to be on the flight deck with the gas crew. There was a lot going on, and it was up in the fresh air. The gas guys were responsible for connecting big, heavy lines to the aircraft just before they were launched. The planes were filled and the lines disconnected. It was an important job. Wisely, the seaman who actually did it made me keep my distance, but it was still fairly exciting. If during the work day any of us middies found ourselves needing a break because we were tired or just plain bored, we just informed someone there that we were requested to be somewhere else and disappeared. No one ever questioned us.

There was a daily schedule issued each morning. We would dutifully report to the assigned place, but when we arrived we just told the person who greeted us that we were needed elsewhere. It always worked. "Elsewhere" often was back in our bunks for a little more shuteye. I suppose this somewhat cavalier attitude toward shipboard life was not exactly what was intended for the first midshipman cruise. A lot of it had to do with the mammoth size of the aircraft carrier. I know that the guys on smaller ships did not have the freedom we enjoyed. On balance, though, we did learn an awful lot about the shipboard life during those couple of months. For several of us, most of whom went on to become jarheads, we learned that we wanted no part of the life of a seagoing swabby.

Deep professional enrichment and appreciation for our naval service aside, our time on the ship was not only fun, but it legitimately helped us to expand our understanding of the world. We traveled to exciting new places with unique and different cultures. Actual work product expectations were minimal, and there was plenty of time to relax. Every day we'd trip across something new, different, or unusual. I will never forget the thrill of the smokers among us when they discovered that their cancer sticks were only a buck a carton or a dime a pack at sea. In fact, several in our group actually took up smoking right then. I guess you couldn't pass up something so cheap that made you look so cool. Most of the cigarettes in those days were unfiltered, and the Surgeon General's report had not yet been issued, although it was imminent. Most of us Marines to be did not take up that nasty habit. We knew we were already pretty darn cool.

The *Wasp* cruise was also designed as a time to build comradery, and in that sense it was wildly successful. Thrown together on that huge metal hulk and left to our own devices, several of us bonded in a way that would never have been possible just walking around a campus. The fascinating concept of "skating," in naval parlance, amused us all. Skating was the practice of avoiding any and all work whenever possible. We all became quite proficient at it. Charlie Pigott was especially in his element aboard the *Wasp*. Never one to hold his tongue if a good laugh was in the offing, he found shipboard life replete with humorous situations. One of his favorite pastimes was to walk through enlisted berthing spaces, which consisted of several levels of hammocks, and yell out at the top of his lungs, "All right, all you squids, get your lard asses out of the rack. Now hear this!" He would shake racks filled with sleeping sailors as he went by and then made sure he was out of the area before anyone really woke up. We were convinced he would do that one too many times and end up rousing up some ex-sumo wrestler with a bad disposition, but it never did happen. His luck held.

Despite the *Wasp*'s gigantic size, when we were underway out in the Atlantic, in addition to a sense of forward motion you could also feel a rolling and pitching with the waves. I don't ever remember anyone being seasick, but quarters were tight, and it was easy to lose your balance if you weren't careful. We would go through the chow line in the enlisted mess and eat at metal tables and benches fastened to the floor, not unlike picnic benches. We drank lots of "bug" juice, more commonly known in the real world as Kool Aid, which was dispensed from central coolers. Since it was a pain to get up every time you needed more bug juice, the next guy up would grab and refill the mugs of whoever needed more of the stuff. On a rolling ship, it took a little dexterity to balance three or four cups on the way back from the bug juice dispenser to the table. Once again, Charlie didn't waste a lot of time figuring that one out. When he was the designated re-juicer, our thirsts tended to remain unsatisfied when he arrived back from the important mission with the refills. As a practical chap who was never especially worried about finesse, he simply carried the refills by gripping each cup over the lip with his thumb and other fingers submerged deep into the liquid. It was so much easier than trying to stick your fingers in those tiny handles. He failed to see a problem with hygiene or good manners. He answered our amused faces with, "Works better that way. I never spill a drop. Whaddaya looking at? I thoroughly wiped last time I went." Only Charlie.

An interesting aspect of the summer cruise program is that it gave us all an opportunity to meet and mix with some of our NROTC counterparts at other schools. You might run into the same guys three years running. Like most things dealing with the Navy, there were good and bad aspects to any situation. I don't want to imply that we stuck-up Ivy Leaguers thought that we were cooler, smarter, and better-looking than the guys from the big state Us from down south, but, in fact, we were. We seemed to get along just fine with our cohorts from Harvard, Cornell, and Yale but had little in common with who showed up from places like Auburn or Ole Miss. To this day, I don't know why a kid from Auburn cannot take a leak without screaming: "War Eagle!" It must be something in the pork bellies they eat down there.

I recall one particular pantywaist from one of the southern schools who struck me as a particularly weak stick. I believe his name was Barry Doberman,; yes, like the dog. He was chubby, dumpy, and totally un-impressive in a uniform. He probably went on to make an excellent naval officer at some desk job at NORAD in the middle of Iowa. It seemed like Barry would just pop up wherever I happened to be and was never reluctant to express his opinion, whether it was asked for or not. I would be going through the chow line, which was obviously staffed by—to be nice—some of the lesser motivated Navy enlisted folks on board. If something ran out, it could be hours before someone bothered to send more food from the prep area.

One evening, I had just gotten off duty from an exhausting fuel crew shift and was sliding my tray down the line. Barry, of course, was just ahead of me. Near the end I spied two scrumptious Jell-O desserts left. One was my favorite, the green. By the time I got to them, though, both were gone; Barry had nailed them both. I wondered if walking the plank was still in the regs. I understand that Barry spent a good portion of our days at sea in sick bay for hives and seasickness. Unfortunately, I will have more on this loser later.

CHAPTER 13

Those Guys Are Good

WHILE LEARNING TO GAME THE system during our time on the *Wasp* that summer kept us occupied, there was a lot more to our shipboard experience than just evading work. Air operations up close, especially involving jets, were unquestionably a thrill to behold. Our Navy pilots are generally regarded as the best aviators from all branches of the services, which is testimony itself that they are the very best in the world. One particular reason is that most of them are carrier qualified, which takes extreme precision, skill, and balls. Landing and taking off from a moving aircraft carrier is not for the faint of heart. The ship is always underway and is bouncing up and down as well. As huge as it is, from the sky it presents a tiny speck in the middle of the ocean. To land safely, the pilot must hit an area no bigger than a driveway perfectly or he'll miss the arrestor cables with his tail hook, which is precisely the reason, by the way, they come in at full power. If the hook misses the cable on a pass, hopefully, the aircraft can regain enough air speed to fly off and go around again. As the pilot approaches the moving flight deck he must keep the red "meatball" beacon glowing from the deck perfectly aligned or he will get a wave off from the flight officer on the fantail. That poor soul tends to frown upon those low landing approaches that threaten to crash into the rear of the ship where he is standing.

As midshipmen, we had heard about all about seaborne flight ops, but seeing the real thing for the first time is truly breathtaking. We watched from an observation deck on the carrier's central island and were transfixed as those tiny, hard-to-see blips way out there gradually become blazing jet fighters rapidly closing in on the ship. Somehow most of the planes roared in and smacked down to catch one of the arrestor cables, which jerked them to an abrupt stop. The cable then unhooks once the plane is safely aboard. Quite often, however, pilots miss the snag and must immediately power up off the angled deck to try again. The noise is deafening, but it is a terrific show.

Jerry Zimmer checking out an A-4 Skyhawk on the flight deck

We spent a lot of time watching the air operations, especially when the jet jockeys were on the program. Needless to say that Charlie and Jerry, who were already future flyboys anyway, were especially fascinated. One bright, sunny, warm and clear day somewhere out in the Caribbean during the middle of the cruise, we were standing on our favorite spot watching the jets return to the ship. Everything seemed normal as the first few planes screamed in and bounced down without incident. Another came in looking a bit high to me. He missed the cables and shot off the angled deck to go around. As we watched, it seemed to take him an extra-long time to wobble out and regain his altitude.

Then, there was noticeable pause in the normal beehive of activity down on the flight deck. Nothing seemed to be happening, and then there was a bone-chilling announcement that echoed eerily over the ship's PA system: "Now hear this. Rig the barricade. Rig the barricade. All non-essential personnel immediately vacate the flight deck."

Jerry looked at Charlie. "What do you think is going on? Is that guy in trouble?" he asked while motioning toward the sky.

Charlie responded, "I'm not sure. Maybe he has engine or fuel trouble, a warning light, or something." Unfortunately, Charlie was right on.

During our cruise, the *Wasp* carried three types of aircraft, which were utilized to accomplish the overall anti-submarine mission of the ship. There was a squadron of Grumman S2F Tracker fixed-wing planes with two high-hung propeller-driven engines. These aircraft were used for extensive over-water patrolling, and had the ability to drop ordnance such as depth charges on suspected enemy subs.

There was also a squadron of Sikorsky SH-3 Sea King helicopters that were also used for patrolling, dropping sonic buoys and depth charges. I actually got to make a flight and go on a patrol off the carrier in a Sea King chopper. The drama associated with helicopter operations is just a bit less than with the jets. The view was spectacular, and, yes, that chunk of metal deck seemed miniscule from up above.

Finally, there was a complement of A4J single-seat triangular-winged attack jet fighters. These A4s had been specially developed for use on the older carriers like the *Wasp*, which could not accommodate the larger jets such as Phantoms and Crusaders. I don't have to tell you that those babies are where the glory boys hung out.

Of course, during flight operations at sea, landing is only half of the equation. Choppers just take off vertically with no problem. The fixed-wing planes take a little more effort. The *Wasp* was equipped with two catapults (starboard and port) at the very forward leading edge of the flight deck. Both the prop-driven S2Fs and the A4s needed a boost to get airborne. The ship would head into the wind to add to the lift. The planes would be attached to a catapult that was retracted to a "cocked" position. The pilot would throttle up his engines, and when ready, would raise his arm to salute the catapult officer. There would then be a huge whooshing sound, a puff of black smoke, and the catapult would rush forward within a grooved track cut in the deck. The plane would literally be thrown forward and released over the bow of the ship where, if all went right, the aircraft's aerodynamics would lift it into the sky. Sitting in a fully powered vibrating jet plane that was about to be tossed off the front a huge aircraft carrier already doing twenty knots or so is also not for the ambivalent. As they say about the PGA professionals: "Those guys were good."

Hanging around the gas shack I heard stories about catapult accidents, but fortunately did not witness one. I was told that every so often, there is what is called a "cold shot." No one is quite sure why, but occasionally there is just no juice in a particular shot. The luckless plane is pulled forward but has no chance to gain enough airspeed to take off. It is just dumped over the bow. I guess that has to be considered a mechanical error. There is also, of course, a human element ever present.

In a few cases where both cats were set up with planes, the pilot on the left gets everything ready to go and hoists his salute. Unfortunately, the catapult officer hits the button for the other cat, where an unsuspecting pilot was nervously waiting but not quite geared up in his takeoff mode. Suddenly, he is shot out. His chances of getting airborne are not very good either. Even during normal launch operations, while we watched the jets from a spot on the island behind the catapults, it was a very frequent occurrence for the plane to be shot and then disappear below the front of the ship. We truly expected a splash any second and held our breath until we finally saw the plane gradually climbing out over the water in front of us. "Those guys are nuts!"

From our vantage point on the island, we knew for sure that the guy going around was in trouble, big trouble. You don't rig the barricade unless there is no other option to bring him in. In an instant, our rapt fascination turned to dire concern. One of those awesome guys in his incredible flying machine had a problem, and we were right there in the middle of it. It wasn't even like going to a sports car race, where the prospect of a crash was always lurking in the background and somehow added to the peculiar allure of the sport. One of our shipmates could be killed right before our eyes. Things felt very personal. Normally the arrestor cables strung across the landing area are configured with hydraulic pistons, which give up to a point when snagged by an incoming tail hook. Any miss was just supposed to result in a max-powered go-around.

Now the bird was wounded and had to come aboard on the next pass. A miss would probably mean a crash into the sea off the angled deck. The system in those days did have a Plan B, if for any reason the arrestor cable system was in doubt. Occasionally, tail hooks broke off, but in this case it was a balky engine. The deck crew was well trained and in a few short minutes, they had erected a barricade across the deck on raised stanchions just forward of the last arrestor cable. The barricade was effectively a web netting with upper and lower horizontal cross pieces and vertical straps spaced at regular intervals across the length. The barricade raised to about twenty feet off the deck. When a plane strikes the web, the fuselage pokes through the web and the wings get caught, thereby transmitting most of the energy into the barricade. If all goes well, the aircraft skids to a stop, ensnared by the webbing. Unlike the cable landings, however, the pilot in this case cuts his power to zero as soon as he hits the barricade. He is an idle "dead duck" if the barricade somehow fails.

After a few weeks, while we still watched the air ops with great interest, we had collectively assumed the dispassion of the old salts we had become. Now, though, all bets were off. Our necks and eyes were frozen, peering into the afternoon haze aft of the ship, trying to pick up any glimpse of the troubled plane. We intensely watched the flight officer in his little pit at the corner of the landing area as he gave signals to the approaching pilot. Finally, after what seemed like forever, we now could see the Skyhawk gradually materializing in the distance. It looked like a giant wobbling bug of some kind with splayed landing gear, wings and tail hook angling out from a spindly body. We held our breath as the plane moved in. For a second, it looked too low and would certainly crash into the fantail. The flight officer coolly signaled some adjustments and, sure enough, the pilot corrected to raise his approach.

"Keep coming! Keep coming!" he urged in a reassuring way.

And then he was upon us. The hazy blip of less than a minute ago was now a fire-breathing, smoking metal monster bashing onto the deck just below us. It was almost surreal when the pilot cut power and, except for the howling wind, the entire flight deck became almost silent. We were used to the S4s landing at full power along with all the cacophony associated with roaring jet engines.

Once on the solid deck, the careening and skidding aircraft abruptly tilted and veered to starboard, where it would obliterate the very ship's island where we stood. Either through the pilot's correction or blind luck, it straightened out just in time. The nose of the plane rammed through the barricade's web on the right side, causing it to bounce, twist, and slide another hundred feet or so down the deck, where the mass of tangled barricade webbing finally brought it to a shuddering stop. Emergency fire and rescue crews immediately surrounded it. The three of us were speechless and finally dared breathe. When we looked down at US Navy Skyhawk No. 305's cockpit canopy, we could clearly see the pilot. Not only was he rendering a smart salute to everyone on board but he had a wide, beaming grin on his face. Guess which one of us thought that was, "Cool!"

Late that evening, long after a scrumptious meal in the enlisted mess, a group of us who happened to be off duty (i.e., everyone) sat relaxing at the rear of the ship on the hangar deck level, gazing out over the fantail. Several were enjoying their new penny-apiece Lucky Strikes or Chesterfields. It wasn't like we had a lot of other things to do. That was way, way before Al Gore invented the Internet, etc.

We must have been heading east because the sinking sun treated us to a spectacular sight as that fiery, molten ball gradually extinguished itself into the placid expanse of green ocean. The Caribbean was calm, and there was just enough of a whisper from the ship's headway to keep us very comfortable on what would have otherwise been a steamy night that far south in the middle of July.

The discussion turned to the emergency barricade recovery. "That guy almost ate it," I offered. "The Navy is obsessed with drills, which can drive me crazy. You wonder why the hell you have to repeat the same stuff over and over. Then you have an emergency like today, and I begin to understand why. You want crews to immediately react and not hesitate to think about what to do. It showed in the response this afternoon."

"They said his engine was running real rough and a flame-out was possible. If that had happened, he would have been a rock in the ocean.

He was lucky he had enough power to do the one go-around so they could rig the barricade," Jerry chipped in.

Charlie added, "There is no question that Navy training and Navy pilots are the best. Marines, of course, go through the same schools. The pilot today was cool. He knew just what to do. I am sure it would have been easy to panic under those circumstances. He was able to keep the meatball steady and watch the flight officer as he came in. That must be pretty tough. I think if it had been me, I would have gained as much altitude as I could, yanked the curtain, and punched out. They could have picked him up pretty quickly in the water after he parachuted down. The guy had big, brass balls. Most pilots probably do."

We were quiet for a few moments, seemingly lost in our thoughts, as we contemplated the gorgeous sunset. It was almost dark. Finally, I was first to speak. "I am certainly not sure yet, but I don't think aviation is in my future. I'll let Eastern and Braniff haul me around. That was just too close out there today."

Jerry absorbed my remarks but decided not to comment, as was his custom from time to time. He did not have to always be the center of attention and remained silent. Charlie, on the other hand, came right back. "Sure, it can be dangerous, but you can get hit by a car in the front of your house. I thought the whole thing was great, and nobody got hurt. I sure don't want to have to land into that clothesline, but I would really like to become carrier qualified. That's the road for me."

CHAPTER 14

Bourbon Street Blues

I T SEEMED LIKE WE HAD been at sea forever when the mighty USS *Wasp* steamed out of the Gulf Mexico and up the Mississippi River delta to the Queen City of New Orleans. We arrived on the 13th of June, ten days after we had departed Beantown. We moved slowly into the turgid, brown channel of the great river, with small mud islands beginning to appear on either side. There was no sign of human habitation but gulls, pelicans, and shore birds seemed to be excited about our arrival. It is a winding trip of over 80 miles from the mouth of the river, and it took us a while, including stops to take on local river pilots. Civilization as they know it in Louisiana began to pop up as we passed the metropolises of Bohemia, Port Sulphur, and Empire. The captain decided not to stop. Gradually, the presence of oil and natural gas production began to dominate the shorelines with a continuing maze of pipes, wells, tanks, and towers lining either shore. Finally, the city itself magically appeared.

After almost two weeks of chipping all that paint and swabbing all those decks, we were certainly ready for a little liberty. I suppose there might have been better cities for a bunch of college kids to visit, but I can't think of one offhand. Of course, we had to deal with a terrible logistics problem when we tied up at the pier. Although we were in the French Quarter at Jackson Square a couple of blocks from Bourbon

Street, the Jax Brewery was directly in our way. We were only there for a few hours when a fire broke out in the beer factory. Having several hundred sailors next door proved to be a lucky break for the brewers. The men on our ship helped quash the flames in short order. As a token of gratitude, the appreciative Jax folks left a beer cooler open for all members of the ship's company at their backdoor. Bourbon Street and free beer; I think I <u>am</u> going to like this Navy life!

After all this time I am not sure that I can recount with any clarity the extent of our on-shore activities, but I am sure we let the "les bon temps rouler." In fact, even if I did remember, I am not sure I would be anxious to recount a lot of what we did. We worked Bourbon Street from one end to the other. Everyone had a "Hurricane" glass from Pat O'Brien's. We listened to jazz at Preservation Hall, ate barbecued shrimp at Pascal's Manale, and even swam in Lake Pontchartrain, which felt like a tepid bathtub. After all, we were a bunch of college kids, mainly from the northeast, who had never traveled very much. At that, it was only a few weeks after finals, and we'd been cooped up on ship. We were ready to blow off some steam. Like we needed an excuse?

In addition to Charlie and Jerry, I spent a lot of time with Jeff Hayes, who was to be my roommate for the next couple of years. Jeff was an extremely bright guy who really had not decided what he wanted to do with his life, but probably even then the Navy was not really in his plans. He loved to have fun, and once told me that all he really wanted in life was to play the guitar, drink beer, and run a hundred yards over bare-breasted women in the surf. While those goals may seem a bit trifling in a sense, what is important to recognize is that we were all still very much kids at that point. There was a large Asian shadow rapidly being drawn over our sun, which we didn't notice or care much about. We were in for some stormy weather, but no one worried about that then.

During that week in New Orleans in the summer of 1963, I recall one incident on Bourbon Street that brings a smile to my face even today. There was a group of us bar hopping that included Jeff, and maybe Jerry and Charlie as well. I am certain that our judgments were sufficiently impaired at that point that we'd dare not drive home. Of course, "home" was that huge piece of gray metal with a gangplank a few blocks away. As our group emerged from a bar, it occurred to me that we had lost Jeff Hayes. It was a mid-week afternoon, and the crowds weren't especially thick, but there was no Jeff in sight. This situation was hardly unusual or troubling. We were standing on the sidewalk discussing which bar to try next when an older, shabbily dressed man approached. He was obviously local and asked me point-blank if that was my friend who had gone into a bar that he pointed to in the next block. His description was close enough, so I assumed it had to be the missing Mr. Hayes. Then the fellow looked me directly in the eye and said, "Do you know what kind of place that is? You'd better get him out of there real quick."

Hey, this was 1963, we didn't even have closets at that time. LGBT? Sounds like one of the Navy's boats. I immediately rushed over and entered the bar, only to find the missing link totally surrounded by a group of very interested men. He was beaming, and when saw me, he shouted, "Hey, Bob! Come over here! I want you to meet my new friends. They are really great guys. The beer is on them all night long, if we want it." He was very indignant when I grabbed him by the shoulder and steered him out the door. "Hey, what are you doing? I just got here!" It was only when I got him outside and several steps down the street that I explained what I had been told about that place. His only pathetic response was a sheepish, "Oh, really?" In a way, I guess he more than returned the favor a few months after the cruise when he played a big part in introducing me to the lady who would become my wife. Jeff, by the way, never did enter the Navy, but he did graduate from Brown. Armed with his Ivy League degree he eschewed Wall Street, choosing instead to try clam-digging on Cape Cod. A few years later, he moved to New York and worked his way into television. He ended up spending fourteen years on the set of *Law and Order*, mostly as the senior executive producer. Not everyone has to be an ensign or second looie.

CHAPTER 15

Banditos in the Honduran Jungle

WHEN THE NAVY WAS CONVINCED that we had done quite enough to help stimulate the shaky Louisiana economy, to say nothing of relieving the pressure on our alcohol-drenched livers, our battlewagon pushed away from the dock and headed back out into the Gulf of Mexico. Our next stop was Puerto Cortes, Honduras. I felt invigorated again to be back at sea, with the salt breeze whistling through my Dixie cup and hearing the reassuring echoes of: "Now hear this! Dump all trash and garbage over the fantail!" a couple of dozen times a day. There wasn't a lot to do, but I guess in the interest of promoting ship harmony and comradery, we were permitted several sunbathing sessions on the flight deck during times when flight operations were not scheduled. The captain graciously allowed us to remove our shirts and tee shirts and lie around on the flight deck to soak up some rays. All those bleached-white, bare-chested men reminded me of a penguin colony. Oh, the USN is wonderful! Shipboard life is for me. How could I ever consider becoming a jarhead?

***Midshipmen at sea (college boys) sunning themselves on
the flight deck of the Wasp, a gracious privilege extended
by the captain. This is not a penguin colony.***

As the Honduran shoreline came into view and the *Wasp* anchored in the harbor at Puerto Cortes on the 26th of June, it struck me that I knew almost nothing about the place. Honduras is situated in Central America between Guatemala to the north and that favorite tourist mecca, Nicaragua, to the south. To this day I do not know why we stopped there. I guess it was a public relations social call. In fact, it was Honduras that inspired the insightful and clever writer O. Henry to invent the term "banana republic." From what I remember, he was right on.

After a little research recently, I discovered that by being there in 1963, we missed the "Football War" with El Salvador by only a few years. It seems that the countries got so mad at each other during a soccer elimination game for the World Cup that a shooting war broke out. Can you believe how ridiculous that was? Why, just look at all the problems we had with the Vietnamese before we barged in. I have been searching for years to find the true reason we invaded Vietnam. Maybe we were sore about a table tennis tournament or something? That still didn't explain why we were now in a bona fide banana republic. In the Navy, it is good idea to go where they tell you. Even if a civil war may break out.

Not only were we going to set foot on the Honduran soil, but the plot thickened. We were instructed to change into our white dress uniforms, which were very reminiscent of the Good Humor ice cream man's get-up. We probably shouldn't have worried, though. I doubt if they had Good Humor service in the middle of Central America. The secret was safe. As midshipmen, we continued to confound all, who couldn't quite figure out who or what we were supposed to be.

The morning dawned warm and humid as we filed off the ship into foul diesel-smelling mike boats that ferried us to shore. We gathered on the steamy, fish-stinking dock area and milled around for more than the required twenty minutes. As is customary in the tropics, the temperature was rising rapidly. A couple of smoky, ram-shackle old busses chugged down the hill to pick us up. We relished their local ambiance for a short ride to a railway station, where we were herded onto rusty old railcars with wooden seats and open sides. So much for air conditioning. The word was finally passed down from somewhere that we were bound for a grand event and party hosted in our honor (?) by the local Honduran government in the city of San Pedro Sula, which was somewhere up ahead in the mountains.

With a belch of black smoke and a muffled whistle, the train lurched forward through dense, lush, verdant undergrowth and jungle. If the train reached twenty miles per hour tops during the trip, I would have been surprised. I didn't know how to say: "Slow down. You'll kill us all!" in Spanish. The heat was stifling, and the view restricted to the thick tunnel of undergrowth and banana trees on either side of the tracks.

After what seemed like hours—only because it was several hours—we reached the thriving burg of San Pedro Sula. Our immediate relief at getting off that smoky, dirty train was short-lived when we soon discovered that the broiling midday sun was an even worse alternative. It appeared that most of the local folk had turned out, and they lined the streets as we walked to the town square, where there was a huge concrete monument to some local hero. I don't recall the natives reacting as if they were especially glad to see us. There weren't many smiles, and no one tossed flowers in our path, but they were certainly not hostile. It was more like when the circus comes to town and parades from the train station to where the big top is pitched. We had the clown suits. All we needed were some elephants. We seemed to be more of a curiosity than anything, or maybe just one more excuse for a fiesta?

Once we had all finally assembled in the square, we were positioned to face a small wooden stage that looked like it got a lot of use. As sweltering representatives of our own great republic, good manners dictated that we at least try to appear halfway attentive to the long procession of local dignitaries and politicians who paraded to the platform to make remarks. If only I'd known how to say: "and in conclusion" in Spanish. Finally, the mayor handed a key to the city to an officer from our ship, and mercifully, the ceremonies were over. Lunch was next, which was a buffet with a lot of spicy things wrapped in leaves, but don't touch the water! Do you know how thirsty we were after that hot, steamy ride and standing out in the hot sun? Wet your whistle now, worry about the trots later.

Despite the heat, I suppose the day so far had been interesting, if nothing else. We had no idea where we were, or when or how we were getting back, but as things turned out, our Honduran hosts had a lot more hospitality in store for us. Later on in the afternoon, we were marched to a large building that was obviously a dance hall of some kind. As we approached the structure we could hear mariachis, violins, and the whole enchilada, so to speak. A dance had been arranged in our honor. How nice! And the operative word was "arranged." As we walked in we were told to line up against the far wall. (Those are orders you really don't want to hear in a banana republic!)

As we stood there, we were astounded to see a stream of young ladies in white dresses file in directly across from us. There were probably about thirty of us and a like number of them. It was remarkable how the grumbling and grousing about the discomfort of the day immediately ceased when a group of interesting females suddenly materialized. They had our attention, and as I recall, didn't look too bad. It had been days since we'd left the Big Easy. They were at least as attractive as most of the townies I had seen back in Providence.

Now for the fun part—San Sula style. The music began, and the lines of boys and girls were instructed to face each other. Each line then moved toward the other one, and you got to pair off with whoever was next in line when your turn came. For once, fate shined upon the guy from Framingham as a very petite dark-haired beauty gracefully took my arm. She was very attractive and had a sweet smile. Obviously, there was a language barrier, but she actually knew quite a bit of English. All of a sudden, this whole day had brightened immensely. Of course, as soon as I whipped out some of my native New England charm, it wasn't very long at all before my babe was off my wrist like a mosquito and flying back over to the girl side. Even with my limited Spanish, I figured out "Adios." I found out later that the deal was, after one obligatory dance, they could take off. I spent the rest of the night mostly talking to the guys and sipping un-spiked punch. In fact, everything would have turned out just fine until I glanced across the room and noticed that my gorgeous ex-date had found a more acceptable partner. I think you already know who it was. Yes, my lovely young Honduran princess had thrown me over for Doberman, of all people! I wish this was not a true story. My ego was crushed—and still is, now that I think of it.

One way or the other, my Latin romance was destined to be very short-lived because at around 2200 hours (i.e., 10:00 p.m. to you civilians) or so, we departed the festive dance hall and headed back to the trains. It was pitch-black as we boarded and leaned back on the hard wooden seats. It was late, and we'd had a long day. I don't imagine too many of us were awake much past the first bumpy mile or two. I remember getting jostled back and forth and breathing that sooty, putrid air, but I was tired and tried to grab a little shuteye.

I am not sure how long we'd been traveling when I noticed that we had come to a complete stop. We weren't moving at all, and were somewhere out in the jungle between San Pedro Sula and the port. I looked up and caught a glimpse of someone riding by on a horse very rapidly There was a quick glint, which I confirmed was a rifle in his hands. And then, all of a sudden, out of the stillness, all hell broke loose somewhere at the front of the train. Gunfire erupted up there. Then I heard a couple of rounds strike the metal roof above our heads. I was very concerned, if not pretty damn scared. Someone yelled: "Everybody down! Now!" I crammed myself down in the seat as much as I could.

What the heck was happening? Was the train under attack? How did we college kids get in the middle of this mess? The bullets stopped, but we heard a lot of yelling up front. I really expected some mean-looking bandito with jalapeno breath to walk down the aisle with a pillowcase to collect our wallets and valuables. We stayed hunkered down as best we could for what seemed like forever but was probably only a few minutes. The night was black, and with the dense foliage canopy over our head, even if there was a moon, the light wouldn't have reached us. We couldn't see our hands in front of our faces. We were helpless and at the mercy of whatever was going on. If only I'd brought that Swiss army knife I got for Christmas.

No one came by to pistol-whip or kill us. No one assured us everything was okay. We were kept in the dark (?). Finally, we heard a very welcome belch from up front and the train began to crawl forward. It still took a few more hours to reach Puerto Cortes, and I didn't sleep a wink of the trip. We were all relieved when we finally arrived at that grimy station where we'd started some sixteen hours earlier.

The USN, by nature, is extremely public relations aware. Bad news travels very fast, and every attempt is made to stifle it whenever possible. Nothing was ever said about our little ambush in the jungle. Officially, it never happened. Later we did hear via the ever-present rumor mill that a gang of bandits did in fact stop the train. Those bullets were real. When someone explained to the band's *jefe,* boss, that we were just a group of American college kids, they were savvy enough to let us pass. They were not interested in incurring the wrath of the US government. Before they knew it, the IRS would be on their tails. Maybe we could have offered up Doberman as a hostage? A side note: Jerry was extremely irritated the next day. It seems that he snoozed through the entire ambush.

CHAPTER 16

"Hey, Chief. Wanna' Buy a Watch?"

OUR NEXT PORT OF CALL was Kingston on the Island of Jamaica, where we arrived on the 1st of July, 1963. If Honduras had left a bad taste in our mouths with banditos and long train rides, the Jamaicans did their best to make us forget any past problems and welcomed us with open arms. By and large, the folks there were merry, gracious, and fun loving. The pace of things on that island was definitely several beats slower than our rigorous intensive shipboard routine. Of course, as soon as we stepped on shore in our white uniforms, we were immediately accosted by a horde of street vendors. So much for stimulating international trade. "Sorry, mon, I love that belt but I am concerned about our country's inverse trade deficit."

This throng ranged in age from young kids to grizzled old men. It was free enterprise and an open marketplace on the most elementary level. If you wanted it, they could deliver it. They immediately solved our identity problem by referring to us as "chief." "Hey, chief, you need a new watch? I have the best there is for only ten dollars." That meant, you could strike a deal for a couple of bucks. "Hey, chief, you want a woman? I get you my mother, she virgin!" There was plenty of that available. Actually, it was a great time to pick up a few souvenirs for the people back home. Let me check my list. Hmm. Let's see. Bongo drums for Dad, a voodoo doll for Mom. Well, maybe I'll wait to see what they have on St. Thomas.

When we arrived in the middle of 1963, Jamaica had just gained full independence by leaving the British West Indies federation less than a year earlier. The favored local dialect was English with a distinctly British twist. My recollection of Kingston, when we first stepped off the dock, was a hodgepodge complex of a large bustling port, industrial complex, and jumbles of white washed masonry residences spread over many neighborhoods, some of which you'd dare not enter, especially at night. It was not too tough to accept the stark fact that Jamaica had led the league with one of the highest murder rates in the world. Kingston itself had little to offer us young college "chiefs."

The bigger island proper, however, was full of adventure and had lots for us to get into. It is a beautiful place, particularly on the northern coast where Montego Bay and Ocho Rios were the more prominent tourist draws. The tropical climate yielded lush vegetation on the small coastal plain that surrounds a central core of small mountains.

A group of us rented a car and somehow negotiated the local traffic and road system some fifty miles across the island to Ocho Rios, where we spent the Fourth of July at the Tower Isle resort. We relaxed and tried to unwind from those two long days at sea from Honduras. We did the beach thing, snorkeled in crystal clear, blue water, and threw back many a Red Stripe, the local brew of choice.

As I reflect back on that visit to Jamaica over a half-century ago, one particular impression has remained with me through the years. Admittedly, I was not yet twenty years old and had not really been outside of New England to that point in my life. The civil rights movement in our country was beginning to heat up, and did burst wide open later in the decade. While I had read about it, I had never observed racial angst firsthand. In fact, I had not even been around many African

Americans. My high school graduating class of over six hundred had just one black student. When I walked around Kingston in my Good Humor duds, I was almost awestruck by the sea of black faces everywhere. It was not that they were intimidating or threatening in any way. It was just that I and my couple of buddies were the only different-looking people anywhere around. For the first time in my short life I experienced a slight inkling of what many black people in America must experience daily. I understood just a bit more clearly what it is like to be surrounded by people who see you as different every day of your life. It can be disconcerting at best.

The US Navy never sleeps, and it almost seems that they would like to ensure that we didn't either. We departed Kingston on July 5 and headed for the final port on our itinerary, St. Thomas in the Virgin Islands, just one more of the world's more incendiary trouble spots. We were forced to endure the white sandy beaches, warm tropical breezes, rum coolers, swimming in azure-blue waters, and feasting on local delicacies. We spent five long days in that hell hole! There was also another feature added to this stop: girls. As a United States possession, the Virgin Islands were thoroughly indoctrinated into our culture and had long been a popular vacation spot for Americans.

We discovered that many young college girls had chosen to spend their summer in St. Thomas, which was something of a pleasant surprise after Honduras and Jamaica. Please keep in mind that this was the early 1960s, and morality had not quite fallen into the toilet yet. I do remember some fun beach parties, boat excursions, and sightseeing with young ladies joining our group. In fact, I even met up with a girl who was in my high school graduating class. My recollection is a bit hazy on this point, but I don't recall hearing about any of us doing anything to suggest that the island group be renamed. Fifteen days after we left St. Thomas in the Virgin Islands on July 24, 1963, we arrived back at the navy yard in Boston where we had departed from some seven weeks earlier.

I would have to think that even in those wasteful times, the *Wasp* and attendant ships could have been put to better use for two months that summer than ferrying a bunch of officer candidates around just to impress them. But it almost looks like that may have been the intention. If our task group killed any subs during the trip, that scoop was withheld from us. The cruise, with all those exciting and interesting places, was terrific for us young, impressionable college sophomores. Except for the actual boredom of being at sea, it would have been hard to set up a more attractive package for us. No one who was aboard, except maybe Doberman, could complain that he had not had the time of his life. Well, then, were we all "gung ho" United States Navy in late July 1963? I can tell you that Jerry wasn't; Charlie wasn't; and I was much less convinced than I had been before the ship ever left the dock.

CHAPTER 17

A Chance Encounter
and JFK

WITH OUR SERVICE TO OUR country satisfied, I now looked forward to a month or so at home to prepare for the rigors of my next year at Brown that would start in September. After such an eventful summer so far, there was not much else of consequence that could happen, was there?

In a move that only was to occur once in my lifetime, my father rented a house on Cape Cod for a week in August. He hated the Cape for reasons that I guess we will never know. In fact, in later life, when considering a final resting place, he absolutely ruled out the US Veterans' Memorial Cemetery in Bourne, Massachusetts. Why? Because it was too close to Cape Cod. That summer, however, we rented a nice little house in Orleans. Fate was definitely in play for me.

It turned out that while we were enjoying our brief stay on the Cape, Jeff Hayes had decided that Longmeadow, Massachusetts, which is in the western part of the state near Springfield, was a little too tame for him. After the cruise, he arrived on the Cape in pretty short order with guitar in hand. We hooked up one evening, despite my father's objections that I needed to spend the rest of the summer with family, and decided to check out the Hyannis Port scene. That area, of course, had skyrocketed in popularity with our new president, John Kennedy, and the family compound they owned there.

We had gone up one side of the main street and were working our way down the other when a blonde on the other side caught Jeff's eye. As luck would have it, said blonde noticed Jeff, and both decided to cross through busy downtown traffic simultaneously. With cars whizzing by on either side they met in the middle of the street. I had followed Jeff, and the blonde's girlfriend had followed her. Jeff convinced Joy, the blonde, to go have a beer with us, and I started up a conversation with her friend. Little did I realize at that moment that I had just met my future and still wife. Jeff and Joy, by the way, fizzled out.

Somehow, I hit it off with this petite girl with lustrous raven hair, gorgeous brown eyes, and a creamy white complexion that had been bronzed by the sun. She was sweet, vivacious, and bubbly. After seeing her a couple of more times that week, we exchanged phone numbers and addresses, but what are the odds? She was Joyce Whitehead from Pittsburgh, Pennsylvania, and was vacationing on the Cape with her friend, Joy. They both worked in the Steel City, which seemed like thousands of miles from anywhere I hung out. Unlike my Honduran princess, however, this deal was not one and done. Joyce clearly recognized a good catch when she saw one. Lucky me. Her sister was married to a guy in the Navy and stationed at Johnston, Rhode Island, a mere shot put toss from Providence. We wrote letters back and forth and when she came to the Ocean State to visit her sister, I got on her dance card. Three years later and many trips back and forth over the Pennsylvania Turnpike, we were married. I can honestly say that was the single best thing that ever happened to me.

The start of our second year on College Hill was certainly a lot less traumatic than the first. We were sophomores (that term still existed in those days), and with renewed "vigah" (JFK) were sure that we knew everything about being sophisticated Ivy Leaguers. After all, we had made it through the difficult year one with acceptable, if not stellar, grades. We were worldly after doing the Caribbean and rubbing elbows in foreign lands. None of us were playing football for the first time in several years, meaning we would have scads of free time to study (right). School should be a snap. A measure of confidence is a wonderful thing, but overconfidence can be dangerous. Personally, the stream of fairly good grades I had earned as a rookie trended down, now that I knew it all. I was never in any jeopardy, but the home office in Framingham was not pleased.

One of the obvious distractions that cropped up in year two that was not around previously was the pledging of fraternities. For a variety of reasons, the Greek system as a US college institution had been under fire for some time. It is much more watered down on the Brown campus today as compared to when we were there. Even in the early '60s, however, Brown's fraternity arrangement was already much more low-profile than at many institutions. Unlike most campuses, the fraternities did not own their own houses, but occupied living spaces connected to independent buffer dorms in the Wriston Quadrangle. Also, I believe very wisely, Brown fraternities did not hold rush meetings until the second semester, and no one could join until their second year. In many other schools, brand-new students were confronted with rushing pressure virtually from the moment they set foot on campus, as if they already didn't have enough other stuff to contend with. At least we had a little time to get our feet on the ground.

Charlie, Jerry, and I all decided to join fraternities, but as it turned out, of the dozen or so available houses, we each picked a different one. Charlie pledged Phi Gamma Psi, which was a solid, well-respected house with the distinct advantage of being located virtually at the Ma Feeney's Rat Factory front door. Jerry became a "Delt" (Delta Tau Delta), which was located next to Lambda Chi Alpha, where I signed on. Lambda Chi was the notorious "jock house," although, truthfully, the Delts weren't far behind. None of us lacked alternatives to join several houses. We ended up, I suppose, where we felt most comfortable. Billy Peters, Paul Kelly, Dave Taylor, and Paul Ryan, all pledged Lambda Chi with me and all also became USMC officers. We lived in the respective houses, enduring the hazing and mandatory nonsense of pledging during the first semester of year two before officially being initiated. Lambda Chi and Phi Gam have long since disappeared from Brown, although I believe the Delts may still be there in some form. As for Lambda Chi, there was very little in the John Belushi *Animal House* classic that I did not witness firsthand during my three years as a brother.

The Lambda Chi brotherhood diligently works on our Homecoming project: "Some Days You Eat the Bear and Some Days the Bear Eats You." Dave Taylor (center) went on to pilot Marine One at the White House for the President.

Contemporary music concerts have always been extremely popular in our society, especially among young people. Even at Brown, way back then, we enjoyed the chance to attend live performances when they were available. As I recall, during our years a number of entertainers actually did come to Brown and put on shows at the Meehan hockey rink or sometimes even Sayles Hall in the middle of the campus, where we met regularly for convocations. These occasions bore little resemblance to the extravaganzas that are popular today, but they did provide a welcome break from the humdrum of studying, especially during the long, cold, dreary winter months. While the Beatles were gathering steam, we were treated to mostly folk singers and musicians, such as Theodore Bikel, Joan Baez, and Peter, Paul, and Mary. I believe I had scratched and skipping 38 rpm records of all of them that I played incessantly on my portable hi-fi in my room. I also was into the Kingston Trio, although they were much too big to sing live at our little school.

One performer who did come to Brown on several occasions was the now infamous Bill Cosby. I remember his opening line one evening as he began his monolog. He gazed out at the sea of admiring student faces, paused to build upon the moment, scratched his chin, and uttered "Brown? Brown? Hmm. What an appropriate place for me to be." His remark, of course, brought a huge laugh from the audience. In those days, the easing of race relations, even at the most liberal school in America, was still just beginning. For many years, this peculiar homespun humorist seemed to offer a unique message that transcended the black-and-white communities.

Of course, Mr. Cosby has fallen from grace in recent times, seemingly for very good reasons. Once a fascinating figure who seemed capable of possibly bridging the gap between the races, his own true "colors," however sad, have become apparent. In fact, Brown was so "down" with the man that in 1985 the university conferred him an honorary degree. Some three decades later, in 2015, the school's governing body, the Brown Corporation, in an unprecedented action, rescinded that degree.

It is difficult to take issue with the university's action in this case. Mr. Cosby has been indicted and is awaiting trial in Pennsylvania.

Almost everyone at some point in his or her life will live through a truly extraordinary event that will in later years conjure up the question, "Where was I when . . .?" The 9/11 tragedy is a most recent example of such a situation. For me, the events of Friday, November 22, 1963, shall go with me to the grave. I remember it as a fairly warm New England autumn day when most of us were looking forward to the Thanksgiving break, just a few days away. I attended morning classes and headed to the Rat Factory for lunch around noon. I was sitting with some of my Lambda Chi pledges when a rumor circulated that President Kennedy had been shot in Texas. I immediately discounted the news. Maybe there was some gunfire? Perhaps he had been shot *at*, but he was so well protected that he could not have been hurt. I was curious for details but not overly concerned as I headed back to my room for the customary few winks before my two o'clock Sociology 101 class. I did switch on my clock radio and confirmed the tragic news that he had indeed been struck by bullets in Dallas. The news was still sketchy and confusing. It was horrible to contemplate, but I was sure he'd be okay, wouldn't he?

I walked to my class and sat there among a group of shocked students waiting for the teacher to arrive. Then the unbelievable word came down: JFK had died. We were in disbelief. Professor Harry Organic walked in. He sat down solemnly without a word and rubbed his temples with his hand. Finally, after a few minutes, he looked up at us and said, "I am very sorry, but I just can't have class today." We rose and filed out, leaving him slumped there in deep thought. I learned later that he had personally done a lot of political work in Texas to help establish a viable Democratic party in that state.

Back at the fraternity house, we talked of nothing else. No one was sure exactly what the death of a president would mean. JFK had not been in office that long. There were mundane concerns, for instance, such as whether or not the NFL and AFL games would be played on Sunday. The AFL cancelled, while the NFL played, and by doing so incurred much criticism. It was all surreal. We listened to the news and stayed glued to our black-and-white television in the fraternity lounge. I was crowded in there with several others the next morning watching live as the alleged assassin in Dallas was being transferred between jails. Suddenly, he was gunned down right before our eyes. We could not believe what we had just seen. Did it really happen? Tragically, yes. And then that shooter, Jack Ruby, himself died in prison about a week later. We were college "kids" but we were growing up pretty fast. Society was changing, but we still had no idea what lay ahead.

It is impossible to speculate with any certainty just what the abrupt change in the White House meant for those of us who were destined to become active duty military officers in a short time, but I am inclined to believe the implications and net effect on us was substantial. Kennedy had been very concerned about our tenuous standing in the world based upon the Bay of Pigs disaster, the Berlin crisis, and other events. He had identified Vietnam as the place where we would take our stand and thwart the spread of communism once and for all. In fact, troop levels in Vietnam had significantly ticked upward under his administration from a few hundred to a few thousand, although no ground troops had yet been dispatched.

He had made a bad bet by backing the Diem government, which was rapidly proving itself to be totally incompetent. Kennedy's rhetoric at the time would still have one believe, however, that he continued to be determined not to commit large numbers of US servicemen to the conflict.

With his passing, Lyndon Johnson took the reins and soon proved that he was not at all reluctant to increase our presence there by huge numbers. Had Oswald's aim been off just an inch or so on that fatal Friday, we can only wonder how many of us would have actually ever set foot on Vietnamese soil. Sadly, we will never know.

CHAPTER 18

Wild Rides in Corpus Christi

AFTER A TYPICAL HARSH AND icy winter, the spring of 1964 brought the prospect of warmer and more comfortable weather. I was discovering that lacrosse, my newfound spring sport, was also played when it was not necessarily nice outside. In Rhode Island, the elements can be very fickle, and snow and ice are quite commonplace in February, March, and even an April storm is not unheard of. In those days, we did not enjoy access to the wondrous synthetic turf fields that are so popular today. Astroturf was just being invented. Coach Cliff Stevenson was a driven sort of guy, and his success running the Brown soccer and lacrosse programs confirmed that he knew what he was doing. He was not about to wait for Mother Nature's okay to begin spring practice. He knew that Harvard and Yale weren't sitting on their duffs.

Our lacrosse practices started in late February on the asphalt parking lot at the Marvel Gym. Much of the time, the coach had the parking lot plowed and cleared of snow, or at least most of it. We had loads of fun slipping and sliding around on the chilly, windy, and frozen asphalt. A few years later, while trooping the infamous "hill trail" at The Basic School, I struggled with shin splint pains on my lower legs, which I attribute to those days of pounding on those hard surfaces in the bitter cold. Jerry was out there with me. At least he got to play in some of the real games, while I watched.

Finally in late May 1964, when we walked out of last final exams with great relief, hoping that we'd be invited back in the fall, it meant that our second class midshipman summer "cruise" was not far off. Yeah! How about Europe and the Med this time? Not so fast, junior, how about, "LANTNARMID," as the Navy fondly referred to it. No big boats this time. It was our turn to visit hot, windy, dusty Texas and steaming, humid Virginia. Sure enough, on June 9, we arrived as a group at the Naval Air Station in Corpus Christi, Texas, for three weeks of flight orientation and training. Decked out in our blue chambray shirts, web belts, bell-bottom jeans, and ubiquitous blue-banded Dixie cups, we were herded around that big, flat base from classroom to hangar to chow hall to barracks. During these marches, Jeff Hayes perfected a 360-degree pivot while throwing a smart salute without missing a step. We were all a lot more amused with his creativity than was the Navy chief in charge of our detail.

At that time, it was evident that the Navy and Marine Corps had high quotas for pilots that needed to be filled. Of course, only volunteers would be accepted. One of the primary reasons for being in Texas was obviously, once again, to encourage us to consider flight training when we were commissioned. It was pretty clear at that point that Charlie and Jerry had fully made up their minds to go in that direction, and they were very interested in the flying portion of our training. Personally, I had an open mind, but Corpus did little to stimulate my interest in becoming a pilot. To me it still had the aura of two minutes of panic on takeoff and landing with hours of sheer boredom sandwiched in between. That said, much of what we experienced during those three weeks was a lot of fun and pretty exciting.

The training schedule provided for us with rides in two types of fixed-wing aircraft and then hops in trainers on a one-on-one basis with actual flight instructors—brave men, by the way. They took us up in the two-engine, propeller-driven S2F Tracker ASW planes, which we had seen operate off the *Wasp*. We had an orientation flight out over the Gulf of Mexico. We were given a lot more instruction about how things worked, but the hour or so flight was pretty small potatoes to us old salt types. The S2F flights were ho-hum events, that is, unless you happened to be Dick Parisen and Bill Droms, two Brown guys who drew the short straw for their flight.

The two of them sat in the bar at the O club that night and recounted their ordeal to a group of the rest of us whom they held at rapt attention. The Navy would have called it a debriefing, or maybe an after-action report.

"We entered the plane and strapped ourselves in that morning, and, as you know, we also were hooked up on the intercom so we could talk to the pilots and listen to the chatter with flight control on the ground," Parisen began as he lit one of his "dimey" cigarettes, took a long drag, and blew out a cloud of white smoke. Parisen was rather smallish and thin with piercing blues eyes that seem to be his dominant feature. He was generally low-key and reserved with a hint of pseudo-sophistication that probably belied his home in Manhattan.

He continued, "The pilot or co-pilot gave us a thumbs up, and we heard the tower clear S238 for takeoff. The plane taxied into position at the end of the runway. We watched and eavesdropped as the men up front went through their final checks. The engine RPMs increased, the plane shuddered, and off we went. We were immediately over the Gulf of Mexico and headed south toward the Yucatan, I guess. The pilot explained some technical stuff to us. It was a beautiful day out there with a blue sky and green ocean. Everything seemed fine."

"Oh, yeah, things were fine all right—for about fifteen minutes," Bill Droms chimed in. Droms made an interesting partner for Parisen on this particular adventure, since he was physically big and chunky. He was known for his quick wit and was naturally outgoing. During this impromptu session, it was almost as if they had rehearsed. One played off the other.

Droms still had the floor. "Here I am, trying to work off a huge tequila hangover from last night down in Nuevo Laredo, and all of a sudden this plane starts jumping and bucking around like we were in the middle of a hurricane. We'd veer to port, drop down, swing to starboard, and crab around. At first I thought these Navy pilots were trying to put one over on us poor, dumb midshipman. Maybe they had a bet on whether we'd use the barf bag or not. Then we noticed that they had gotten kind of quiet up front. When I asked them if everything was cool, no one responded."

Parisen picked it up. "Yeah, I had never been in one of these planes before but all the bouncing sure didn't seem right. These babies are made to cruise for long hours on patrol over water. Surely they couldn't act like this during those flights. I was getting concerned by their silence, if nothing else. I could see we were heading basically out to sea. I couldn't even break out the butt I desperately needed. Finally, one of them spoke. 'Men, make sure your seat belts and harness straps are good and tight.' That was reassuring all right. I think I'd prefer the silent treatment."

"Straps, hell, I began to think about a parachute, but somehow we'd missed that part of the class," Droms added. "And then things got worse. We heard the pilot click the mic and speak over the radio."

"Base this is S238. Do you copy?"

"Roger, S238. How can we help you?"

In a voice as calm and steady as a gentle breeze through a royal palm tree the pilot replied, "Base. We have a situation here. We are not in a May Day status yet, but we do have a problem controlling the aircraft. Our main rudder tail stabilizer control seems to be out. We get no response from the flight deck. It seems to be loose and causing us to pitch and roll as it flaps around. We seem to be able to maintain our altitude but cannot effect a good turn either direction. Oh, and you are aware that we have LANTMIDs on board? Please advise."

"Holy shit!" Parisen almost shouted as he sipped his beer and puffed on his cigarette. "May Day, I know what that means. We are bumping and jerking and headed straight out to sea. How much gas do we have? How far is Mexico, Florida, or Texas? It suddenly got very hot in there. We were both really sweating it. We were helpless. All we could do was say a prayer and hope the guys up front were good."

Base came right back. "We copy your problem, S238. We have scrambled you some company, who should join you in a few minutes. We have you clearly on our screens. We will keep all other aircraft out of the area. We have notified the Coast Guard, who will deploy their assets in your direction. Please try to remain at between 3,000 and 4,000, if possible. If you are certain that your rudder control is totally out, we suggest that you try dual engine alternate feathering protocol. Are you familiar with it?"

"Roger, Base. Confirm, no rudder control. We've done that maneuver in the simulator but never for real. We will give it a try and see if it works."

"Simulator! Bill and I were glued to the sides of the plane. Every time it swooped down, we were sure it was the end and we were going to crash. There was nothing we could do. I will say one thing, I never saw or sensed any panic in the guys up front. They remained unruffled and steady—or maybe they just had us fooled. I looked outside after a while and saw an A4 Skyhawk arrive on our starboard wing. He obviously could not get too close because we were flying so erratically. I wasn't sure what his mission was. Maybe shoot us down or something? Just seeing him, though, was a little reassuring."

Finally, the pilot spoke to us. "Okay, gents, I want you to hold on tight. We are going to try something to turn this baby around and get you home for lunch. I sure don't want you to miss that. Okay?"

"'Ya, yeah, yes, sir,' we replied in unison and held our breath. We watched them feverously working the controls."

Droms broke in, "Bullshit, Parisen. I had my eyes shut."

"Okay, Bill. Well, anyway, all of a sudden we heard one of the engines slow way down. I think it was on the port side. The other one seemed to pick up at about the same time. The plane did start turning. Our heading was changing. There was only one problem; the plane had banked way to the left and headed straight down toward the Gulf's green water. We were careening at a sharp angle rapidly toward the ocean. The smooth, green carpet below quickly became covered with ripples and waves that were getting larger and larger. I don't know our altitude, but I could sure see the whitecaps. We were still tilted severely to port as we angled down. I really didn't think we were going to make it. The sea was rushing up. I was sure we'd had it. Why had I wasted all those hours studying for the Econ final?"

"I was bracing for impact, when suddenly the other engine roared to life. The plane seemed to hesitate, then buck and lurch up. My stomach was now in my mouth. Very, very slowly, the aircraft began to climb and straighten out. I would not have been surprised if the bottom of the fuselage was wet. It took us a little while, but we gradually reached our slotted altitude. The plane continued to buck and yaw, but now we were at least headed back toward NAS Corpus. I could breathe again. Talk about needing a smoke!"

Droms had to add, "I am sure happy I didn't have to face an underwear inspection that afternoon." That cracked us all up.

"The pilot asked us if we were okay and even had the balls to ask us if we wanted to do that again. He went on to explain that without a rudder, he could not control the direction of the aircraft. He had employed a procedure whereby using the two engines and feathering one while goosing the other he could kind of control direction that way. We were headed back to the base. As long as he could get a good alignment on that big, wide runway, things should be fine as far as landing was concerned. He was right on that score. There was big reception party for us when we landed without a problem. Fire trucks, ambulances, service trucks, the whole bit. I would never want to go through that again, but my hat is off to those terrific pilots. They never panicked or lost their cool. You can keep your flying. Where's my big sturdy battleship?"

All is well that ends well, of course. It was very interesting to us at the time that the incident was never mentioned again by anyone in the Navy. We were instructed not to discuss the matter with anybody, especially the press. The last thing the brass wanted was for the media to find out that two of their fair-haired college midshipmen had almost deep-sixed over the Gulf. Aviation is inherently dangerous. Military accidents do happen on occasion with some frequency, despite all the care and caution in the world. It really does not make sense to highlight those type of events.

Grumman S2F TRACKER ASW Patrol Plane

June 1964, Third Class NROTC cruise to NAS, Corpus Christi, Texas (from left John Stabb, Bill Droms, Jeff Hayes, Dick Parisien, Charlie Pigott). Droms and Parsien took the white knuckle fight out over the Gulf.

CHAPTER 19

Full Assault on
Virginia Beach

IF THE *NORMAL* S2F ASW patrol flight was tame, the jet flight was a real buzz. During the second week one morning we boarded an old two-engine transport plane, which covered the short distance over the south Texas savannah from Corpus to Kingsville in less than an hour. The Navy air facility at Kingsville was used for jet training, and we were in for a treat. Each of us was paired with a flight instructor. The Navy at that time was using a Grumman two-seat fighter aircraft known as the F9F-8T Cougar, as the primary training aircraft. The plane was powered by a single jet engine positioned in the center of the fuselage. It had been active in the fleet since the early 1950s and was eventually phased out entirely by the early 1970s. A few of them made it to Vietnam.

I know that Jerry and Charlie would have agreed with me that jet jockeys do things with just a little more style than their prop and helicopter brethren, and that morning it sure seemed to be the case. We got to sit in the front seat, with the pilot directly behind. You could talk to him but not see him. It was really cool to get up on the wing, being very careful where you stepped, to enter the cockpit with the canopy pulled back. The planes were painted white with red tails, noses, and part of the wings. We had gone through a class about ejecting from a jet aircraft, and that thought was certainly not appealing as we began to taxi. All you had to do was grab the ring just behind you and pull the curtain right over your head and stay compact. The ejection seat would do the rest. Sure!

Four planes taxied out together and took off in rapid succession. To this day, I cannot believe the power and exhilaration you feel as the thrust explodes and drives you into the sky. I am talking about a plane about to be mothballed fifty years ago. I can't imagine how powerful the later ones must have been. We flew out over south Texas and the pilot put us through some basic maneuvers—barrel rolls not included. There were times during that flight when I had no idea what was up or down and was totally disoriented. Kind of like a few fraternity parties I had attended.

Everything was so much quicker and faster than the prop planes. We flew over the naval gunfire range in a deserted area of cactus and sagebrush not far from the Mexican border. I could see some bombed-out tanks and other targets on the ground. We made a semi-pass, but did not drop any ordnance. Ironically, some forty years later I hunted deer in that very same area. In fact, I even found a live .50 caliber round that had probably fallen out of a plane.

The jet ride was really too short, but I still remember my neck being snapped back as we approached the field in the proper pattern, which called for paralleling the runway and then breaking back with two 90-degree turns to line up and bring it in. After that flight, I certainly could appreciate the romance of a jet aircraft, and the allure of sitting in the pilot's seat. For the first time, I clearly understood, at least in part, what drove my friends toward those magnificent machines.

The balance of our time in Corpus was spent in what was actually beginning flight training. We were each given as many as four hops with certified, for-real flight instructors. The training plane at that time was a North American Aviation T-28. It was a two-seater, single-engine, propeller-driven aircraft and was widely used as a trainer for all the services.

We were given instruction as if we were already in the program. We became familiar in all the checks prior to takeoff including Preflight, Start, Pre-taxi, Engine Run Up, Runway, and Takeoff. Once in the air, we were given the stick to actually control the plane in flight. Eventually, by the last few flights, we were almost taking off, doing touch and gos, and landing by ourselves. I enjoyed it, but did not come away feeling I had really gotten everything down. My mouth dropped when Charlie told me that his instructor was ready to let him go solo in a couple more flights, maybe the sixth or seventh. Of course, those flights never happened, but I guess I should not have been surprised.

It would be difficult, if not impossible, for me to leave discussion of our time in Texas without at least touching on the liberty. Corpus Christi was a nice enough community even then, and we did visit the area's beautiful beaches. The real attraction, though, to a bunch of college kids was, of course, Mexico, since it was just right across the border. Well, maybe not quite "right across." The closest town in Mexico is Nuevo Laredo, which is a drive due west across south Texas of about 150 miles. It is easily within striking distance for a weekend jaunt but tough on a weeknight.

Back in the early sixties, life was truly far simpler than is the case today. There were no cartels, murders, kidnappers, walls, or generally bad guys around back then. They wanted our Yankee tourist dollars, to be sure, but you could come and go from that delightful country pretty much as you wanted. It is certainly more complicated today.

A group of us made the obligatory trip to Laredo over the first weekend we were in Texas. We found a cheap motel on our side and crossed over the bridge into Nuevo Laredo where we hit every bar and curio shop within striking distance. We all had to have a sombrero. During my preparation for this book, I came across a snapshot of a man leaning against an adobe wall taking a siesta in Mexico wearing a big sombrero. The caption says it is Jeff Hayes, but it sure looks like a local hombre to me.

Texas, by the way, at that time had some pretty backward laws concerning alcohol consumption. Many counties were completely dry. An 18- or 19-year-old being able to buy a beer was not always a given. That was definitely not a problem in Mexico where we could chug cerveza to our hearts' content. And, yes, candor obliges me to admit that there was also another strong attraction to the place for young, virile males—the cat houses. Nuevo Laredo, in particular, was the home of Poppagayos, a house of ill repute with quite a repute far and wide across the border. It must have been on every AAA list of things to see and do in Laredo. Although I cannot and will not swear to the whereabouts of many of the guys on our trip, please be assured that neither of my two jet-jockey-to-be friends or myself went anywhere near that institution.

What is the old saw? Join the Navy and see the world. After three weeks of parading around the hot, dusty plains of south Texas, where there were often no trees to spoil the view, we were off to the steamy palmetto and cypress swamps of the Tidewater in southern Virginia. According to the information we received at the time, we had already learned about the importance of "SEAPOWER" in our academic studies. We were now about to learn how "the amphibious Navy-Marine Corps Team projects its mobile power ashore from any place on the seven seas." There was a "FOUR-OCEAN CHALLENGE" facing us that the NAVY-MARINE CORPS TEAM was specifically geared to meet. Bluejackets and Marines worked harmoniously every day of the year to make amphibious landings happen. Well, sometimes.

Once again we climbed aboard a Navy transport in Texas and landed in Norfolk, Virginia. Starting on July 1, we spent the next three weeks at the Naval Amphibious Base at Little Creek. Overnight, we went from cool Navy flyboys to trained killer Marines; well, not quite. There were Marines around, for sure, but the idea was to understand amphibious warfare. The Navy provided the transportation and the Marines took the beach. That's kind of like, "I'll drop you off. You go in and rob the bank." Obviously, the division of labor is a little out of balance. There was lots of classroom time, both in and outdoors. We sat on bleachers and watched a full-scale landing put on by real Navy and Marine personnel. We also did some calisthenics and ran around some trying to act like Marines, I guess.

The culmination of our amphibious warfare training was to make a landing of our very own. At some point during this training, even we sophisticated Ivy League snobs actually had to break down and admit that some of this stuff was just plain fun. Down deep every kid wants to play soldier sometime in his life. Nobody was shooting at us, but we could go charging off the landing boats onto the beach, screaming and firing blanks from our M14s like we were all John Wayne clones. In fact, I really had to admire the southern schools guys who came equipped with their own battle cry (e.g., the sickening Auburn "War Eagle"). At Brown we had nothing comparable. Maybe we could have invented something like the "Bellicose Brownies . . ." or maybe not.

We trained for about a week on cargo nets and in mike landing boats. We studied invasion tactics and strategy. The day before the invasion we were ferried out to a troop ship, where we spent a hot and sticky night. At o'dark thirty we prepared our equipment and assembled in the pitch-black. At the designated time, the order was given and we crawled down fuzzy cargo nets into bobbing, really smelly diesel-powered mike boats. You've seen them forever in WWII movies. They have high sides and a ramp that goes down in the front when the boat hopefully reaches the beach. There have been many, many instances when the boat hit a sandbar still pretty far out and the ramp went down, only to have the invaders step off into twenty instead of two feet of water. It seems a little humorous until you realize that most of us were wearing fifty or sixty pounds of additional gear.

The mike boat rides can hardly be compared to the swan or duck boats at the Boston Public Garden. In fact, the time you spend crammed like oysters into one of those ugly sculls seems to last forever. First of all, they plod through the waves so that you feel every bump. Even if you are not prone to sea sickness, your resolve will be thoroughly tested when the guy next to you blows his breakfast. Then there are diesel exhaust fumes that are absolutely stifling if the wind is wrong.

Mike boat drivers are renowned for getting lost and delivering their guys to the wrong place. Even if everything else goes okay, it is not at all unusual for the mike boat to circle or wait in position for what seems like an eternity until the signal to land is given. At that point, you would offer anything just to jump overboard. Of course, all that unpleasantness is quickly forgotten when the effort is for real. The real fear factor cannot be diminished. There is simply nowhere to hide when that ramp comes down. Maybe the Navy makes it so uncomfortable on the ride in that the men become so desperate to get off, that even a frontal assault on a reinforced machine gun emplacement does not seem so bad.. All kidding aside, my esteem for the troops who landed at Normandy and other similar places during WWII is immense.

In our case, we hit the beach, the ramps went down, and we charged off firing blanks from our rifles like crazy. Lacking any opposition, we were successful in "taking the beach." Our landing was hardly the Super Bowl of events, but I guess we all got the idea. Our stay with the amphibious folks passed quickly. Weekends in Virginia, including the Independence Day holiday, were spent on the sand at Virginia Beach. The lure of beer and babes is always a wonderful panacea for anyone who is bored. On July 22, 1964, we were released, and headed home for what we could scrounge up of the remaining summer vacation before school started again in the fall.

CHAPTER 20

"Don't You Know That Marines Get Killed, Son?"

NEW ENGLAND DOES NOT HAVE the reputation of being an especially warm and cozy place, but there is nowhere else on earth where I would prefer to spend my autumns. The seasonal switch from summer sizzle to fall fizzle has always been a particularly welcoming event for me. Even though I know that the icy winter blast is not far off, I have always felt invigorated when the leaves begin to turn and a nip is in the air. This feeling of exuberance was even magnified if you were so fortunate to spend it on an elegant college campus, such as Brown, where the vitality of the place merges with the symphony of the season. As I returned that fall in 1964 to begin my third year, I began to awaken to and appreciate many things that I then-to-fore hadn't even noticed. Perhaps subconsciously it began to dawn on me that it wouldn't be too long before this collegiate joy ride would end, and I would be compelled to deal with the real world. The excuse of being a dumb new college kid didn't fly anymore. I was beginning to grow up.

On the other hand, I do not want to leave the impression that overnight I was transformed into a "West Quad weenie" who studied twenty hours every day and seldom came out from under his rock. That was certainly not the case. I still had plenty of time for fun and games. It was

131

just that my perspective was changing a bit. Academically, for instance, the third year was the point at which you began to work earnestly in your major, which presumably would connect you to a profession of some kind after graduation. The Brown curriculum at that time was very restrictive, with virtually no options outside of the arts and engineering. A business concentration, which I would have preferred, was not offered; although, strangely, Egyptology was available. Charlie and Jerry both ended up as economics majors, which was about as close to business as you could get. On the other hand, I chose sociology, and was quick with the explanation that since I was unsure at that point what I wanted to do after college. Sociology was sufficiently broad that it allowed me a lot of latitude. Well, it was very interesting, and also not the most rigorous of majors, I will freely admit. How else would I have been able to take a course most popularly known as "Nuts, Sluts, Queers, and Peers"—the Sociology of Deviant Behavior? Looking back now at the '60s, maybe I was on to something.

During that fall, all three of us were occupied with getting comfortable in our majors, NROTC drills, mediocre football, fraternity activities, and a general pursuit of the haute social life that the Brown scene generously offered. I suppose that there is a college campus in the country that does not have at least one college restaurant/bar where students can enjoy a beer or ten. I am sure even BYU has such places. Back in those days, with a legal drinking age at a totally unreasonable twenty-one ("you can go off and fight for your country but you can't have a beer or vote"), such places were a little harder to find. Necessity, of course, is the mother of invention, and we didn't have to venture too far to find a shift-working, second-job barkeep who thought we all looked legal. Our establishment of choice was the Crystal Tap, which was located right down the bottom of College Hill next to the bus tunnel on the edge of downtown Providence. After a few hours of relaxing, the "bus only" tunnel was a frequent shortcut on the way back up the hill. The ambiance of the Tap was clearly more blue-collar-worker oriented than adorned with college boy décor, but we weren't particular.

Talk about cheap butts on the ship; well, believe it or not, the place served ten-cent drafts of that local nectar of the gods, Narragansett beer. "Dimey" drafts will bring us in every time. How many evenings did I spend sipping dimey drafts, playing bumper pool, and enjoying breaded quahogs on the half shell? Sounds pretty good right now. I never was quite bold enough, however, to try one of those boiled eggs in green, murky Seekonk River water in the glass jar on the bar.

I am sure Jerry and Charlie patronized the Tap from time to time, although I cannot recall ever seeing them there. I do remember us discussing another famous Providence culinary landmark, Mike's Diner. In fact, I personally recommended it to them as "the" place to dine when in the city during late-night hours. Mike's had four metal stools of the old drug store variety fixed to the floor with round and spinning vinyl seats. Mike's was truly a mobile operation, even before Steve Jobs. The entire place was on wheels and was towed every night about 10:00 p.m. into the parking lot next to the Providence train station. Magically, it disappeared before traffic picked up the next morning. There may have been other items on the extensive menu, but I never got beyond the franks and beans with thick brown bread. (You know I never consulted their wine list.) Talk about delicious! We would visit Mike's after a few hours of getting warmed up at the Tap, which was only a few blocks away. Often, in those days before plastic money, we left the Tap because we were "tapped out," so to speak. No one had any cash left. That was not a problem at Mike's. It was so small and so crowded around 1:00 a.m. that people were lined up and pushing three and four deep for every seat. You would wait your turn, gobble your beans, and politely get up to let the next hungry guy sit down. A little squirming and jostling and you were out the door. Did I forget a step in there somewhere? Alas, all good things must come to an end. During our senior year, Mike's trailer hitch snapped on the way up College Hill, and the rolling beanery was smashed into obscurity.

The Crystal Tap was the mood creator and departure point in a somewhat unfortunate escapade during my junior year. As bad as Brown was in football, we were pretty darn good in ice hockey. In fact, while I was there, the team actually made it to what they now call "The Frozen Four." That fateful evening I had attended a game against Boston College, which we mockingly referred to as "Notre Dame of the East." We didn't like those genuflecting holy rollers with an attitude. After the game, and reassuring myself that my studies were in order, I ended up at the Tap with fellow fraternity brother Bob Gregg. I had been Bob's "scutt" during pledging the previous year. Bob was not a big guy but was wiry and well put together. Although soft spoken, when pressed—or after having a few—he would back down from no one. He claimed he was strong because of all the clams he had dug up on the beaches at home on Long Island.

After concluding our business at the Tap—which probably meant we were out of cash—we drove up the hill in my father's green Volkswagen bug that I was permitted to keep at Brown. We had every intention of calling it a night.

As I turned around the corner, the unthinkable happened; an empty parking space popped up on the street right next to the Wayland Arch, which led right into the Lambda Chi house. Parking spots on the street around the congested campus were scarcer than *A*'s in the classroom. I was feeling pretty lucky, although I soon found out it was other than the good variety. As I was fumbling with my seatbelt and getting ready to open my door, I glanced over at Greggsy, who had somehow become engaged in a heated conversation with someone standing in the dark on the street. That "someone" turned out to be a BC Eagle, and a pretty big one at that. Before I knew it, Bob's door opened and he was forcibly yanked out of the car. My dimey haze notwithstanding, I was alert enough to surmise that something was very wrong. I quickly jumped out on my side and found myself surrounded by several big, ugly guys from Boston, who for some reason did not seem pleased. I think we had won the hockey game. Maybe that was it?

My rapid summation of the predicament was that my best odds were to attempt some diplomacy, until I looked over my shoulder and saw that poor Mr. Gregg was getting the tar pounded out of him a few steps away. And then to add insult to injury, I was certain that my eyes were deceiving me. My mouth fell open as I saw that the door to my father's little car had been completely ripped off and was lying in the street. It was sort of rocking a little bit in the glow of a street light. To this day, I have no idea how that happened. Based on these two new bits of intelligence, I quickly opted to abandon any thoughts about diplomacy. I was pretty sure that I was about to suffer the same fate as my buddy unless I seized the advantage. Without any warning, I swung from my heels and caught the closest ape squarely in the jaw. I suppose I should have hung around for a damage assessment but decided instead to seek help. Without excusing myself, I bolted for the Wayland Arch and through the door into the frat house. Needless to say I had a group of BC animals close behind me, apparently interested in an unscheduled tour of the Brown campus.

Sometimes, it takes a crisis to appreciate how others see you. I was to get a quick read on how I was perceived among my friends; not that I was known to joke around or anything. I burst into the corridor of the Lambda Chi house with the Boston thugs in hot pursuit. I flew around a corner and with relief saw a group of my brothers sitting in a room with the door open, playing cards. Reinforcements at last. As I ran toward them I desperately screamed, "Help me! Help me!"

They barely raised an eyebrow. One of them looked at me and deadpanned, "DeLuca, be quiet. We are trying to concentrate here."

"No! No! Seriously, you idiots. I'm in big trouble. I need help!" Still, no one moved. So much for my creditability.

An instant later, my pursuers came thundering around the corner and charged up the hallway. Frustrated, I pointed. "See! Those guys are after me!"

Finally, it sunk in. The cards went flying and the jock house contingent jumped up and stormed out after my assailants, who had wisely turned around and hustled back the way they came. Once outside, those nasty guys had disappeared into the night, although it took all my doing to keep my brothers, who were now ready for blood, from pummeling John Davis, a Brown student and friend of mine who had happened by to help us. Bob Gregg emerged slightly worse for experience and sported an impressive shiner for the next week or so.

With the hostilities over, I now faced the unhappy prospect of calling my father and telling him about his wingless little bug. Dad had a well-earned reputation of not always being the most understanding person, but in this case he was terrific. He asked only one thing, "Who won the fight?" After assuring him that his son had prevailed, he was fine with the whole thing. Boys will be boys, I guess.

The world was rapidly changing around us as we diligently went about our metamorphosis in our university student cocoons. After four years of gestation, when we finally emerged ready to fly with our degrees, we would be confronted with a far different place than existed when we began the process four short years earlier. Many of our long-held beliefs and ideas had been cast away. It was getting increasingly difficult almost daily to determine the bounds appropriate decorum and open public display.

One evening that fall of 1964, I and a group of my fraternity brothers were glued to a transistor radio in our lounge as brash twenty-two-year-old Cassius Clay boldly jumped into the ring in Miami Beach to take on the "Big Bear," Sonny Liston. Clay had been verbally baiting Liston for several weeks, and none of us gave this big-mouth upstart even a slight chance in the ring with this huge, chiseled world champion monster. It seemed impossible that this green young kid would do any-thing but get mauled by this intimidating winner of thirty-five of thir-ty-six bouts. The somber and mysterious Liston came off as the epitome of invincibility and meanness. Clay had to be scared to death to take on the heavyweight champ who looked hard as a rock, with a nasty scowl that never left his face.

We all expected a quick KO, but somehow the bold kid hung in there well into the fight. And then, to our astonishment, the champ did not answer the bell for the seventh round. A traditional icon was dead, and a new, free-spirited replacement had rudely tossed him out. That amazing boxing match proved to be a true harbinger of many things to come.

The year 1964 was also when the Surgeon General's first report was released that conclusively linked lung cancer to smoking. The Beatles had all but arrived and made their epic appearance on the Ed Sullivan show. Jeopardy premiered on NBC. (It is still going strong. I guess not *everything* has changed.) The first draft card burning took place to chants of "We won't go." President Johnson signed the Civil Rights Act of 1964. Nelson Mandela was imprisoned. The first Ford Mustang rolled off the assembly line. Three civil rights workers were killed in Philadelphia, Mississippi. LBJ won a landslide victory over Barry Goldwater. Bob Dylan was becoming popular, and the Beach Boys were at the top of the charts.

While all these events were noteworthy and impactful in their own way, there was another significant happening that year that probably had more direct impact on the Brown NROTC students than anything else. On August 7, acting upon incomplete and unconfirmed intelli-gence that North Vietnamese attacked a US destroyer in open waters, Congress passed the Gulf of Tonkin Resolution, which gave President Johnson virtual unlimited authority to wage war without further con-sent from Congress. And wage war he did.

For some of us in the NROTC program, our junior year, which spread over 1964-1965, was the time to make a critical decision that would certainly affect our lives from that point forward. If you were so inclined, it was necessary to select an option and be accepted for commissioning into the United States Marine Corps instead of the United States Navy. I never knew if there was a specific USMC quota, but about a fourth of us did opt to become jarheads. For Charlie and Jerry, I do not believe the choice was very difficult at all. In my case, the decision was not as clear-cut. After what I had seen of the Navy, shipboard life was very unappealing. On the other hand, I was not certain that the Marine Corps was a good fit. Unlike some, I had never even really considered the Corps before I went to Brown.

A complicating factor in my decision lay at home. My father had been an officer in the Coast Guard, and I think he just sort of assumed I'd end up in a blue uniform with gold braid. A Brown graduate and WWII veteran, he was categorically against the Marines, which frankly, kind of characterized his negativity with respect to many organizations. He had a penchant for finding fault without being able to see any good. He would root against a football team in any particular game instead of having a favorite. On one of my weekends at home, I screwed up my courage and broached the matter with him.

"Dad, I have been talking to my friends in the unit, and a lot of them are considering the Marines instead of the Navy."

He thought for a moment while he puffed on his ever present acrid-smelling pipe. "So? What do you want me to do about it?"

"Well, I have also spoken to Major Charles Webster and Staff Sergeant Ron Benoit, who are regular Marines assigned to the unit. I really like them. They are very impressive men. I can't say the same for many of the regular Navy officers I've met. Major Webster told me he thinks I'd make a great Marine second lieutenant."

"I am sure he thinks that," was the comeback. "He obviously has a tough quota to fill. He has to attract as many people as he can. I have always said the Marines have the best press agents. They know how to toot their own horns. They love to brag and show off, but there isn't really as much there as they'd want you to believe. The Navy has problems, too, but at least they are not too big for their own britches. You are in the *Navy* ROTC. The Navy has paid your way through Brown. Stick with them. You don't need those stuck-up braggarts."

"I have made one cruise and I was bored to pieces most of the time. The Navy is out to sea and away from family at least half the time."

"Have you ever thought about the casualty rates of the Marines and Army in combat? It can be very dangerous. There is nothing like a nice, safe, clean ship way out on the ocean."

"That was true, Dad, most of the time—in your day. Have you thought about the guided missiles they have today and what an easy target a lonely ship can make?" The subject was dropped, and we picked up something else to argue about.

The more I thought about it, the more I was intrigued about taking the option. The Navy did not excite me, although I was sure I could get along fine if that was the way things worked out. There was no way I would join the Marines just to avoid the Navy. The Corps, though, was a different story. It was exciting, and several of my good friends, including Charlie, Jerry, Billy Peters, Paul Kelly, and Dave Taylor, were all going to become Marines. Jeff Hayes was not, but he was at that point going to be lucky if he graduated at all. I suppose I just needed a little push to get me over the top and then wage war with my father.

Well, I don't suppose it was really a push, but when I really sat down with Major Webster and Sergeant Benoit, there was almost no convincing left to do. They both told me that I would make an excellent Marine. They had been observing me for a couple of years and had long had their eyes on me, along with the other guys who were signing up. They knew I had played football and lacrosse and was certainly strong and tough enough to prosper in the program. They had a very respectful way of making me feel wanted. Their pride in their organization was very apparent. I left wanting very much to serve next to men like that.

I met Major Charles B. Webster when he was in his mid-thirties. At slightly over six feet, he did not cut the lean and hard image of a squared-away recruiting Marine. He was clearly rugged and strong but had a unique approachability. He exuded a friendliness and warmth despite his impeccable appearance. Upon meeting him, you could not help but notice his piercing blue eyes. He looked at you when he spoke and listened intently when you talked to him. Charlie Webster made it immediately obvious that he was very interested in what you had to say. His door was never shut, and you could always count on him for good cheer and a fine sense of humor. Charley Webster left Brown before we graduated, and as a lieutenant colonel, took over the 3rd Battalion, 5th Marines in Vietnam. His command played an instrumental part in Operation Cochise against the 2nd North Vietnamese Army Division. He served with exceptional distinction, which was no surprise to me.

Gunnery Sergeant Ronald E. Benoit was a career Marine and Vermonter, who was assigned to work for Major Webster at Brown. The SEALs and Green Berets get a lot of well-deserved credit, but you rarely hear much about the comparable USMC team, the Force Recon men, who are every bit as outstanding and perhaps more so than the comparable groups in the other services. Ron Benoit was Force Recon. He was not a large man, standing a few inches below six feet. Even in those days he had a balding pate with closely trimmed dark hair on the sides. He had bushy, dark eyebrows and slightly droopy eyes. Out of uniform, you might mistake him for somebody's brother, rather than the hardened Marine that he was. He was instantly personable and very easy to get to know. Clearly, he could be hard as nails if the situation warranted, but he normally came across as outgoing and affable. He enjoyed his time at Brown, and was very prideful of his Corps. He understood his job, but would be damned before he'd let a weak link slip in under his watch. He loved the Corps and was not embarrassed about showing it.

After leaving Brown, Ron Benoit went on to distinguish himself in combat as few have ever done. For his valor and heroism in Vietnam he was awarded the Navy Cross, which is second only to the Medal of Honor as our nation's highest award for valor. According to his commendation on the 25th of February, 1967, then a second lieutenant serving as commander of a recon platoon, he was inserted by helicopter into a hot zone that was mined, booby-trapped, and surrounded by the enemy. Exposed to withering enemy fire, he waved off a second group about to land, organized his men, tended to the wounded, and called in artillery strikes. After becoming almost completely deaf from a booby trap, he guided in medevac and other choppers to evacuate all his men. He was the last to leave. I stand in awe of this man and his accomplishments.

I was all but convinced to opt for the Corps, when, after one of our drill sessions, I walked back across the main campus from Lyman Hall to the Wriston Quad with Jerry and Charlie. It was chilly and brisk, with the cold, bitter winter not far off. The subject of the Corps occupied our conversation.

Jerry was never one to beat around the bush. "Well, Bob, have you signed up yet? What are you waiting for? Come on, get with the program! You'll do great in the Corps. What do you say?"

Charlie's assault was also of the direct frontal variety, although his tactics were a little bit different. "Yeah, Eight Ball, get off your butt. Are you really thinking about hanging around with those Navy squid when you graduate? It takes a real man to be a Marine. I can't believe you haven't committed yet. Get your ass in gear! Come on, we'll have a blast in Quantico next summer."

I really needed no more convincing. I was determined to become a Marine and join these great people. Surprisingly, my one anticipated major obstacle at home offered no objections to my decision. I am not sure why, but I think he was flattered that his son had been recruited by some very impressive people. It must be a good deal. I immediately went by and signed my option, which evoked a smile from Jerry and additional razzing from Charlie. I have never, ever, regretted that decision.

CHAPTER 21

Love Conquers All

THE SECOND SEMESTER OF OUR junior year flew by. I was preoccupied with studies, Lambda Chi, playing lacrosse, the Brown Key Society, and working at the Meehan Auditorium officiating intramural ice hockey games. It was now 1965, and it didn't seem to be a very big deal when in March, LBJ sent the first ground troops to Vietnam, but it really was significant. The Rubicon had been crossed. Escalation was on.

At the NROTC Unit, we talked about these things, of course, but that war still seemed very far from Providence, Rhode Island. Our space program at NASA, which had been thoroughly drubbed and embarrassed by the Soviets, was beginning to show signs of catching up with successes in the Gemini program. Civil unrest was rapidly boiling over in the crucible, and finally exploded with the Watts' riots in Los Angeles.

In general, real and permanent societal evolution and change tends to be very subtle. You observe individual events and incidents, which at first seem isolated, extreme, and way out of the norm. Not too much time goes by and you discover that certain types of formerly abhorrent behavior have caught on and are being accepted in large segments of society. Protests, hippy culture, long hair, free love—all were creeping into major segments of our society. Much of this stuff, of course, was not lost on us. Skirts were getting shorter and hair was getting longer. The Beatles, Grateful Dead, and Stones were everywhere. Our societal values were teetering but had not yet toppled. Free love was yet to come. Damn!

By the time we arrived at Brown, for all practical purposes, the institution had been coeducational for many years. Pembrokers attended classes with us and were very much involved in virtually everything that happened on the campus. Despite an abundance of testosterone-driven joking and amusement among many Brown male students concerning the attractiveness of the archetypical lady, the proximity of Pembroke gave us a wonderful social resource. Even though my very own mother was a Pembroker, for some reason I never did avail myself of this immediately accessible cornucopia of dating candidates.

Once again, Charlie Pigott, however, was not shy about helping himself to targets of opportunity. His freshman beanie had hardly been hauled away by the trash collectors when he met a special young lady in one of his classes and embarked upon an extraordinary relationship that would endure for the rest of his life. Carol Crockett came from Concord, Massachusetts, which is only a short musket shot from my home. Concord, of course, is best known for its role with Lexington in the Revolutionary War. Her father was an accomplished author and sometime educational TV personality. *Crockett's Victory Garden* was a very popular and successful book on gardening. I believe her dad even had a series on National Public Television along the same lines. Kid all you want about females at Pembroke; Carol was a catch. I remember her delightful, laid-back demeanor and easy affability that made her pleasant to be around. Her sparkling brown eyes and glistening brown hair added to her appeal. An outward reticence and bemused expression at times belied her profound intelligence. She possessed a wry sense of humor that made an interesting contrast to Charlie's outward bravado. Their relationship bumped along for the first few years and eventually they moved off campus together as seniors. Marriage was not permitted under the regular NROTC scholarship program, but theirs was not the first instance where love trumped law.

Jerry Zimmer took a different route to find and woo the lady who was to become his eternal soul mate. Like me he ignored the "somewhat" deep talent pool only a few blocks away at Pembroke and chose to look elsewhere. I am not sure that love at first sight has any applicability but, as Elaine reports, after their first date, neither ever dated anyone else. It looks very likely that pretty early on, Jerry knew that he had found "the" one. As always, when Jerry wanted something he would pursue it all ahead full.

Elaine, who was born in North Providence, had moved to New Hampshire, where she spent her formative years, and only moved back to Rhode Island after high school graduation when she enrolled at Bryant College, right next to the Brown campus. As fate would dictate, there was a girl in Eldridge Hall, where Elaine lived at Bryant, who had gone to high school with Jerry in New York. That girl asked around if there was anyone who would be interested in meeting Jerry. Elaine's name came up, and, even though Elaine was somewhat hesitant based upon the wild reputation of the matchmaker, they did meet .It was Jerry's first semester of his sophomore year and Elaine's very first semester at Bryant. A love connection ensued.

Jerry and Elaine were in a steady relationship when Elaine graduated from Bryant in two years with an associate's degree. Some twenty years later she completed her formal education; a degree in journalism from San Diego State University. While Jerry completed his senior year, Elaine took a position at Brown, at first in the Admissions Office, and then later as an administrative assistant with Dean Anne Stewart, who was the dean of students at Pembroke. Elaine adored Dean Stewart. Although Elaine and Jerry never moved in together, she was able to see him on a regular basis. She understood that he was headed for the

Marines and a military life, at least for the first few years. Jerry spent his free time working parking cars and attending preflight ground school in southern Rhode Island.

Elaine, of course, has some very interesting memories of their courtship and time at Brown. On one occasion during Jerry's junior year, they attended a formal NROTC ball or similar event of some kind. As luck would have it, the finalists for the revered title of "Prince and Princess" came down to Elaine and Jerry and her roommate, Nancy Davis, who was accompanied by fiancé Len Caldwell, also a member of the NROTC unit. When the band paused before a hushed audience and a drum roll echoed across the room, Bert Parks (remember him?) solemnly tore open the secret envelope and announced that Elaine and Jerry had won.

Apparently, Nancy was not so thrilled for her roommate's good fortune. Elaine recalls their friendship pretty much ended after that, as did their living arrangements. Boys will be boys, but sometimes women . . .?

I was amused to note that Jerry tended to be very possessive during the course of their dating, which Elaine was told by Jerry's mother was a common familial trait. I am hardly surprised; when Jerry set his sights on something, he would not rest until he achieved his goal. They were married in the break just after graduation and before The Basic School.

During my life, if there has been one consistent and recurrent pattern to my behavior, it is that while I almost always get to where I am going, I almost never do it the easy way. If the kid's bike has a left and a right, I will inevitably assemble it backwards the first time. And so in romance, I could not find anyone suitable in virtually the entire northeastern part of the country. I decided to wander far afield, and ended up with someone who lived over six hundred miles away. Ours was a Pennsylvania Turnpike relationship. On several occasions during breaks and holidays, I boldly thrust my thumb out into oncoming traffic and hitchhiked that long and seemingly always cold and snowy trek from

Providence to Pittsburgh. If you do not think our country has changed, just think about a college guy trying that today.

We dated for a year, after which I gave her my fraternity pin, and then took the big step with a diamond a year later. We did the same as Jerry and Elaine, and officially tied the knot between graduation and The Basic School.

CHAPTER 22

OCS: What Have I Gotten Myself Into?

As they say in the NFL "upon further review", I had abandoned ship and was now a confirmed Marine officer candidate. By the way, one of the very first bits of advice that any NROTC-USMC option receives is to take a look at his blue paycheck. It still does indeed say "United States Navy" on it. Like it or not, we are still a part of that organization. There is a tendency for new Marines to look down on the mother service and cast aspersions in that direction. We were assured by USMC lifers that was definitely in bad taste. Why bite the hand that feeds you?

Anyway, insulting the Navy was the very least of my concerns as we shook off the winter chill and eagerly awaited the temperate spring balminess. The end of the semester would bring my first real test as a Marine, at Officer Candidate School (OCS) in Quantico was fast approaching. I hoped I was ready.

To the typical man on the street, the most widely held impression of the United States Marine Corps is the classic boot camp scene where a razor-thin, hard as nails drill instructor wearing a Smokey the Bear hat chews the tails off a quivering squad of bald recruits. It is a fact that the general idea of most basic military training is to break down the recruits and then build them back up the way you want them. The

Corps takes this approach to the extreme to ensure that only the tough-est, fully qualified, and best will make it. Many fall by the wayside. The start of every Marine's career is designed to be a living hell for the first several weeks. When this period of intense harassment is finally over, the survivors appreciate that they have really been through a very dif-ficult stretch. Incredibly, despite having been beaten down by the harsh and bitter treatment, their self-confidence and pride swell accordingly. Therein lay my challenge—getting from Point A to Point B. It was not going to be fun. I had to be ready. What had I gotten myself into? Was it too late? Maybe staring into a blinking radar screen on a bouncing ship was preferable to grappling with pugil sticks.

All kidding aside, I was convinced that the next six weeks were go-ing to be among the most difficult and rigorous of my life. The Navy's laid-back, resort-like atmosphere was long gone. For most of my life, starting on the playgrounds in junior high up and through my first three years at Brown, the aura of the United States Marine Corps was a constant in any related conversation. Boot camp was a rough and tough experience. As young college men are wont to do, we built it up to the point where it seemed larger than life. It was going to be a real test of physical and mental stamina. Yes, we were NROTC punks, in which the government already had a substantial investment. They certainly did not want us to fail, but very likely, some of us would. The price of failure for an NROTC regular was steep. Not make it through OCS and in all likelihood, you could plan on at least a couple of years mop-ping a deck somewhere as an enlisted seaman recruit. That would be the horror of horrors.

As I traveled down to Virginia for the NROTC version of OCS, I was apprehensive, but I honestly believed that I had what it took. The terrific staff at Brown sure seemed to think so. I promised myself only one thing: if for some reason I did wash out, I would have given it my very best effort.

Our home for the next several weeks was the second floor of a typical austere wood-frame barracks building on the base at Quantico, Virginia. A "squad bay" in those days consisted of a rectangular room with a painted concrete floor, containing two rows of about two dozen Marine-green metal upper and lower bunks. Each man had a wooden foot locker for his personal items. There were curtain-less windows on both sides, and ceiling-mounted fluorescent lights overhead. Each bunk was made with one also Marine-green blanket pulled so tight that you could bounce and catch a fifty-cent piece off of it. The sinks, toilets, and showers were located at the center of the building. That area was particularly popular at 0530, with about a hundred guys all wanting in. The place was designed for absolute functionality. Comfort or personal privacy had no part of the equation.

When we reported in earlier in the day, we were processed through a warehouse building where we were issued all the clothing and personal items we would need while we were there. The nice scowling gentleman directing us through also made sure that our hairstyles were "event appropriate," and summarily buzzed our heads down to almost bare skin. I don't remember him asking me how much he should take off the sides. I think the guy was a sheep shearer by trade, moonlighting on the base. We then took all our clothing and gear back to the barracks, where we attempted to stow it exactly in the prescribed way. When all the officer candidates had arrived by late afternoon, we were ordered to fall in for our first formation in our utility uniforms in front of the barracks. It was show time.

A big difference at OCS as compared to The Basic School later on was that even though at certain times the programs resembled each other, in The Basic School we were actually commissioned officers, however green and wet behind the ears. We were commanded by fellow captains and majors. Not so at OCS. As Marine option officer candidates, our standing was less than nothing. We were under the complete and total control of non-commissioned officers (i.e., career sergeants) who liked nothing better than heaping it on us privileged college boys. It started immediately.

A gunnery sergeant moved to the front of our assembled company. He stood well over six feet and looked like he'd been cracked out of a superhero mold. His utility uniform was smartly pressed, with creases that looked like you could shave with them. His spit-polished boots beamed in the fading afternoon sun. There was just a hint of hair under his drill sergeant hat. His uniform and demeanor were so perfect that he could have been a manikin standing there. He glared at us for a moment with a look of disgust on his face, as if we had already pissed him off. He then boomed out in his best drill instructor baritone, "Company! Atten-Hut!"

Our huddled mass instantaneously reacted as we stiffened and came to attention. The gunny then proceeded to lay down the rules for the next several weeks. Everything was to be done at double time. Everyone would always be on time for everything. No one had better be late, ever. He and his staff would direct us around when we were in formation, but there would be times when we would be responsible to get places on time on our own. Every morning we would fall out for PT with the daily dozen exercises and a run. It was back to the barracks to shower, and then off to chow. We would not miss chow. There would be unannounced barracks inspections. Lights out would come at taps. Every man in his bunk. No exceptions. There was a demerit system. Earn a few and you could forget about any liberty for the next six weeks. We needed to work and study hard and would be judged on three things: leadership, classroom, and physical conditioning. Everyone would not make it. Only the best get to serve in this man's Marine Corps.

There was no opportunity for questions. We were still at attention when he did a smart about face and individual DIs moved in front of each platoon. The intimidation game was on. Our man was obviously from somewhere in the south, based upon his distinctive twang. I will call him Sergeant Tucker, although his real name escapes me after all these years.

After briefly introducing himself, he carried out our very first inspection, during which he proceeded to tear us up one side and down the other. He moved with a swagger and approached the first man in the first squad. In a tone that closely resembled a roar, he called out just about everything I could think of from un-shined boots, to wrinkled uniform, to gig line amiss, unpolished belt buckle, wrong tee shirt, need a shave, long hair, need a shave again, unblocked cover (hat), and on and on. The rest of us stood by erect and stiff, waiting for our turn in the barrel as he moved down the line. He was clearly in no rush.

Sergeant Tucker was not a tall man, but looked all the part of the tough and seasoned drill instructor that he was. I was in the second squad near the end. Charlie was in the first squad in front of me to my left. I could hear the sergeant moving down the line towards Charlie. The proper response to any question directed at you by a DI is always followed by: "Sir! Yes, sir!" in as loud and manly a voice as you could muster. And you'd better know the answer to the question, by the way. I heard many a meek "Sir! Yes, sir!" as he moved toward Charlie. Then he was in front of Charlie, who was probably a foot taller than the guy. Charlie, by nature, was not a slob, but he also was not necessarily the neatest person you'd ever meet. After the sergeant worked over candidate Pigott pretty well, he let fly with a question I certainly wasn't expecting.

"Okay, mister!" the eagle-eyed NCO shouted. "How old is the United States Marine Corps?"

Charlie did not even pause for a second and screamed right back in his gruffest, toughest voice, "Sir! One hundred eighty-nine years of hell, death, and destruction! Sir!"

The sergeant hesitated and looked Charlie up and down again. He didn't speak, but I am sure I saw the smallest hint of a grin on his face.

He then abruptly turned to chew on the next man. Charlie Pigott; there was no intimidating him.

OCS did not disappoint, and turned out to be all the fun and games we had anticipated. The staff did their best to keep us hustling around and off balance as much as possible. Our morning runs were increased from one mile to three or four. Almost always on the runs and forced marches, a few guys got so gassed that they fell out. By doing so they offered up raw meat for the instructors' voracious appetites. While I was not fast, I never had any problem running distances. In fact, I enjoyed running. I don't know how many times the squad bay lights would be rudely switched on at 0200 and we would be ordered to stand tall in our skivvies for a surprise inspection. As irritating as these sessions were at the time, we knew it was all a drill and should not have been a surprise to anyone.

There were many hours in the classroom learning USMC history and traditions, as well as some basic small unit tactics. We marched everywhere and had close order drill sessions on the parade deck almost every day. Compass and orienteering was a primary topic. I'll bet today, with the advent of GPS technology, recruits wouldn't even know what a compass is. We ran a field exercises out in the woods, where we were given several azimuths to follow to navigate from point to point. At the end of each leg there was a painted metal ammo box with a number on it. You recorded that number and moved on to the next spot. At the end you turned in your list of numbers, which hopefully matched the course you had been given. The concept was easy, but doing it was another matter. I remember being quite confused during that exercise. There seemed to be boxes everywhere and people wandering in all directions. I am pretty sure that the unusual proximity of the moon that month affected the little round floating circle in my compass.

Weapons training was another big part of the program, especially the proper use, care, and cleaning of the M-14 rifle and .45 pistol. The

M-16, the controversial next generation rifle, had not yet been introduced. We spent lots of time field stripping and cleaning both weapons. In theory, you were supposed to be able to field strip your weapon blindfolded. After a while, it became worse than the most boring preacher you have ever had to sit and listen to on a Sunday morning. Hours after hours after hours listening to a DI explain, re-explain, re-re-explain, and then re-re-re-explain the proper cleaning, assembly, re-assembly, and use of those weapons. Appropriately, there was an uncompromising emphasis on safety, which was also drummed into our heads. As incredibly dull as that instruction was, the fundamentals have actually survived with me today as a hunter and owner of firearms. I sincerely wish my own sons could have gone through that part of our course.

The military, out of necessity, obviously orients such basic teaching approaches, especially in the personal weapons area, to the lowest common denominator. They assume that if they get through to Private Shmuckateller, the dullest bulb, perhaps most everyone else will catch on. Repetition, therefore, is a vital element in their training methodology.

Nowhere is that more woefully apparent than in boot camp on the rifle range. In those days, the USMC taught four basic firing positions: off-hand (or standing), kneeling, sitting, and prone. Proper basic body positioning is critical for each one. To drive this stuff home, our company was taken to a hill that resembled a large earthen amphitheater with no seats. We were distributed evenly around each level with our rifles in hand. A sergeant below us in front on center stage led us in practicing each of the four positions, while other instructors walked around the levels to assist and correct. These thrilling sessions were affectionately known as "snapping in." We had no ammunition and had to visualize a spot off in the distance and pretend that we were actually firing. We weren't allowed to say "bang" though. We practiced this inane stuff for hours and hours over two or three excruciatingly long days. You have no idea how agonizingly monotonous it was to endure this rote stuff, especially with temperatures well into the 90s. I guess I shouldn't complain too much. I was told later that at the real enlisted Marine boot camp they "snapped in" for an entire week! Maybe our college educations did give us a slight benefit of the doubt. They should at least change the name to "napping in," which would be more on target, so to speak.

After all the proper safety, care and cleaning, and snapping in, we were finally permitted to fire live ammunition at the real rifle range. We fired off hand, which is the toughest from the 200 yard line, sitting, and kneeling from the 300 yard line, and prone from the 500 yard line. It was critical that a shooter adjust his sights for the effects of wind and elevation as he moved back to each new yard line, or as the instructors called it, getting the right "dope" on your rifle. Of course, not everybody remembered to adjust when they moved to a different yard line.

We shot at circular targets with concentric rings radiating out from the black bullseye in the center. There were Marines hidden in the butt area just below the targets. Once a shooter on the line had finished cranking off a volley, which impacted into the dirt just above their heads, they lowered the target and marked the spot of each hole so the shooter would know his score. A complete miss earned a "Maggie's Drawers" which was a wave of a red flag on a wooden stick. You sure did not want to see many of them. Every Marine was supposed to qualify annually using a rifle and his table of organization prescribed weapon, which was for us, the .45 caliber pistol. We didn't actually fire to qualify until The Basic School. The OCS drill was strictly to learn. Even before I actually became a hunter, I always felt pretty comfortable on the firing range.

As I have mentioned, at OCS we were living and operating in an environment where every little misstep was jumped upon and magnified by our guards, errr…instructors. Learning and using the proper military lingo was critical, of course. One of the most egregious, yet very common, sins that a candidate could make was to refer to his rifle or pistol as a "gun." "They are weapons, Mullet!" A "gun" was something else. During our enthralling "snapping in" exercise, one of our group, who I believe might have been Dave Taylor from Brown, committed that dreadful, inexcusable mistake within earshot of a DI. Dave was a wonderful guy, who approached most things in life with a bemused grin on this face. He never seemed to take himself or much of what was going on around him too seriously. This time, though, he had gone too far and there was penitence for this sin of all sins. He was ordered to run four laps around a nearby track, holding his rifle high in the air and grabbing his crotch. During his run, he had to keep repeating for all the world to hear "This is my rifle. This is my gun. This one's for shooting. This one's for fun." I suspect Dave didn't make the same blunder again.

One of the most memorable inclusions on our schedule was the obstacle or "O" course, which we visited frequently. The course back in those days was a straight line one hundred yards or so from start to finish. Long before the current American Ninja Warrior craze, this course was designed to test speed and conditioning but not necessarily stymie individual Marines. All the obstacles were fairly easily negotiable. The course included low hurdles, an up and over bar, a wall, combination obstacle, and fifteen-foot rope climb. The combination obstacle had hand over pipes, log walk, and high rollover log. It was interesting to watch guys as they moved through the course. Some of the innately gifted natural athletes, like Billy Peters, gracefully moved through it seeming to barely slow down at all. Jerry Zimmer was also quite proficient on the O course, where you didn't have to necessarily be tall. Charlie was a bull, who attacked the course and battled his way through it. In my case, I have always had good endurance to run distances, but speed and upper body strength were not my strong suits. Although I could knock out fifty pushups and a hundred sit-ups, maybe five chinups was my limit. I actually did fine on the course until the rope climb at the very end. I struggled mightily, and often did not make it to the top. I certainly heard about that from the kindly personal trainers in the Smokey hats. Later on, by the time I got to The Basic School, I had worked very hard and had mastered the rope climb. When I was given enough rope I did not hang myself.

One of the final culminating events that faced us during OCS was a long forced march within a fire team (four Marines) up and down over trails through the woods. We wore helmets, carried full packs, rifles, and equipment. An instructor (without gear) accompanied us to observe and also to throw impediments in our path, like, "He's wounded!" or "Incoming!" We trekked several miles in the heat, and it was pretty testing. I felt our group came through it pretty well. I remember setting the pace for much of the march. We were asked to give peer evaluations on how we felt each other had performed during the exercise. I have no recollection of who was in my group, other than there was no one from Brown. It was a true test of endurance and toughness, and I thought we had done okay. I was to learn shortly that apparently not everyone shared my opinion.

It was just after lunch on one of the final weeks of the program when, as I returned to the barracks, a note was handed to me to report to the company office at 1300. I was puzzled, and when I arrived there were about five or six other candidates there as well. We stood cooling our heels while the rest of the guys hustled by for the afternoon formation. As Jerry passed by he asked me what was going on. All I could do was shrug. After a few minutes, they started to call us in one by one. When my turn came, I entered an office with a first lieutenant sitting at a desk. He told me to stand at ease but did not motion me to take seat.

I was very puzzled as I stood in front of him while he silently read from paperwork. He finally looked up and said, "I have reviewed your record since you have been here, and there is some question about you remaining in the program. How do you feel about it?"

The USMC is not known for subtlety, but I was blindsided? It was like a ton of bricks had been dumped in my lap. I was stunned. I immediately thought back about anywhere during the past few weeks where I might have had trouble. All I could think of was the rope climb. I was not aware of anything else that had been a particular problem, any more than anyone else. I stammered back, "Sir, I am very surprised. What have I done wrong; or, what haven't I done right?"

He glanced down at the sheet in front of him. "As you know, you are being judged on three things: academics, leadership, and physical conditioning. Your academics are fine, but you had trouble with the O course. Also, your peer evals for the forced march were low, which reflects on your leadership scores. You are marginal in both areas."

Now I was really at a loss. The forced march? Huh? "I am sorry, sir. I have always had trouble climbing a rope, but I am working hard on it. I guess I can understand the PT part of it; but the other was not something I could have guessed."

He looked up and stared intently at me. "I see. Tell me, Mr. DeLuca, honestly, do you want to remain in the Marine Corps program?"

I suppose he had to ask that question, but my answer was short and to the point. "Absolutely, sir."

He continued to stare. His eyes never left mine. "Okay, then good. We are required to warn anyone who may be in jeopardy of not making it through. You have your warning. You may return to your platoon. You are dismissed."

I made some gesture to thank him and stumbled out of his office. I was thoroughly confused and shaken. What had just happened? Deep soul searching was inevitable. Maybe I *am* kidding myself and don't belong here. I caught up to my platoon sitting on bleachers and listening to a lecture on grenades. I certainly didn't hear much of what was said.

After evening chow, we were back at our squad bay. Jerry walked over and asked me again about where I had been. I told him about my meeting.

He was incredulous. "You have got to be shitting me! You have been doing great. You have never fallen out on any run or forced march. The classroom stuff is a piece of cake. I don't get it. Maybe you just pissed somebody off. That happens. Don't worry about it. You are going to make it just fine. The USMC needs you. Suck it up. Forget the whole thing."

And, you know, with Jerry's encouraging, I did manage to put all that aside and graduate from OCS with everyone else. I am not sure I could have done it without his reassurance. I never knew him to be anything other than positive and upbeat. In fact, I never heard another word on the subject, although I am sure my rank in that OCS class was closer to the end than the top.

As I described above, I selected the Marine option in no small part because of the quality of the people in and around the program. That fall, back at Brown, I sat down with Major Charley Webster and openly discussed my OCS summer vacation. He gave me some advice during that conversation that I will never forget.

"Well, you know, Bob, in anything like that with many people involved, the only ones who really stand out are the few at the very top and very bottom. Whether you are in the upper twenty-five percent or lower twenty-five percent really doesn't make a damn bit of difference. You made it through. That is what counts. Now go out and have a great career."

CHAPTER 23

The Bug Rolls South

IT HARDLY SEEMED POSSIBLE THAT we were now in our fourth year since that auspicious afternoon on the football practice field when we heard the Carrie Tower toll marking that splendid victory over Colgate. Not that Brown's football fortunes had changed all that much during our tenure on College Hill. Including the two-win season in 1963, over four years we enjoyed eleven gridiron triumphs, which computes to almost three per year; still, pretty heady stuff for the Bruins. Had Jerry Zimmer, Charlie Pigott, and I remained on the team, however, I am confident that the fortunes would have been far more bountiful. For us, football was already far in our rearview mirrors. In fact, we were much more preoccupied with other matters, principally, we had to finish growing up. No longer fuzzy-faced eighteen-year-olds, we had reached our majority and could now drink and vote, not that we had ever been much bothered by the first of those matters anyway. In retrospect, it is sobering to note that while we could finally consume alcohol and cast ballots, notwithstanding that, we had reached the age where we could fight and die for our country several years earlier. Legality aside, in truth, we had matured immeasurably, and there was little question that much of that development was attributable to our summer cruises and exposure to the military. We were about to be booted out from under the comforting college-boyhood shelter of the past four years. Not all our classmates were ready, but I know three who were.

Unlike many, many of our contemporaries, the three of us had been extremely fortunate in the arduous selection of a soul mate. We were stable, yet driven, young men, who happened on three terrific ladies fairly early on in our college careers. All three relationships involved long courtships. Elaine and Jerry, and Joyce and I planned to be married right after graduation and commissioning. Charlie and Carol took a little different approach, but, once again, that was Charlie. That fall in October, I made a trip down College Hill into Providence to meet my uncle Ralph, a local CPA, who could "get anything for me wholesale." He knew a jeweler who would get me a deal on a diamond. We went up to the second floor of an old office building on Weybosset Street into a cramped old shop where I plunked down $275 for a diamond ring. I have no clue where I came up with the cash. Wait, upon further review, I do remember. Another Lambda Chi, Soupy Campbell, and I ran a football pool around the fraternity houses. I proudly plowed my net ill-begotten gambling profits into her ring. When Joyce arrived for our big fall weekend, I made her an offer which she apparently couldn't refuse. Unquestionably, it was the best investment I have ever made.

Despite all the imminent distractions, we all paid enough attention to the business at hand, which was to wrap up our studies with enough credits to be assured that we would be invited to walk through the Van Wickle Gates at commencement in the spring. While it didn't seem like much of an accomplishment then, how many college kids obtain their degrees in four years wire-to-wire today? The answer is, not many. Charlie was especially active as a senior as the president of Phi Gamma Delta, president of our Semper Fi Society Marine Club, and as student battalion commander of the NROTC unit. Somehow, I was elected as the "High Epsilon" of Lambda Chi, or social chairman, which was unquestionably the most demanding and unappreciated job anywhere. I guess my brothers knew a pigeon when they saw one.

As I have described above, the fraternity system at Brown, while not quite on life support during our years, was definitely headed in the wrong direction. On many large state school campuses, fraternity membership was truly a big thing and a very valuable credential to ensure maximum social life enrichment. At Brown, joining a frat was hardly necessary. Fraternities, though, were fun, and many of the friendships I made there still exist to this day. I am not sure about other houses, but our Lambda Chi chapter had more than our quota of colorful characters. Early on in my pledging days I became friendly with brother Ed Marecki, who was a year ahead of me. I first met Ed in connection with the NROTC unit where he had selected the USMC option, as I eventually did. Unfortunately, much to his regret, Ed suffered an eye injury that disqualified him from further participating in the program, and he had to drop out. During his time at Lambda Chi, I have heard Ed referred to by an array of affectionate sobriquets, but Ed was best known as "No-Neck Mareck." He was built like the classic fireplug, with scant variance in physical conformation from head to toe and was 100 percent solid bulk and muscle. His USMC aspirations ended, but he did graduate and go on to have a fine career in business; that is, after he had become a legend around the Lambda Chi house.

As irresponsible but nonetheless creative fraternity brothers, we were always on the lookout for especially nutty behavior among our brotherhood. Ed provided ample fodder for us and won the coveted distinction as "the grossest guy in Lambda Chi" for three years running. Sunday morning debriefing sessions after Saturday night parties were always filled with Ed's adventures. We all learned to cover our ears around him or be subject to a wet finger appearing out of nowhere. Perhaps his signature event occurred while he was attending dinner with several senior faculty members and the dean of the Sociology Department in a private dining room. In anticipation of the event, Ed had done his homework. In fact, he performed an exhaustive multi-volume survey of the sociological implications of the likeness of the Indian on the Narragansett bottle label. Hunters and gatherers are frequent fodder for discussion among sociologists. Perhaps in retrospect, though, he may have over-prepared and arrived a bit too fortified for the affair. Despite a noble attempt to make constructive contributions to what had to have been very stimulating conversation, partway through the meal our hero swooned and passed out at the table, much to the mortification of his fellow diners. Fate at least was somewhat in Ed's corner that evening in that his sudden nosedive propelled him squarely into the mashed potato dish, thereby easing his landing and possible nasal abrasions. Rumor has it that ingots of the resulting spud-driven splash soiled and ruined a silk tie worn by the dean, although that detail has never been confirmed by eyewitnesses.

After Ed graduated, I thought it only appropriate that we create an award named in Ed's honor to be placed in our fraternity house trophy case along with all our intramural sports awards. One trip down the hill to Providence and I returned with a non-descript fake marble Little League trophy and joke shop plastic hand flashing the victory sign with the middle finger. A little Elmer's glue and gold paint, and I unveiled the "Edward P. Marecki Grossest Guy in Lambda Chi" trophy. I placed it prominently with all the other awards in the glass case in our lounge, to be handed out in the spring at the end of the school year to the most deserving brother. I was proud of my work and was certain Ed would have been thrilled with this august recognition.

I was still in school, and it really hadn't dawned on me that some of the behavior that was routinely accepted in our frat was not necessarily condoned out in society, especially in a business environment. Oh, well, live and learn. After graduating, Ed had been hired by a Fortune 500 company, Rigel Paper, I think, as a management trainee. And wouldn't you know it, we hadn't been back at school in the fall for more than a few weeks when who shows up in his impeccable three-piece suit, white shirt, red print silk tie, and spit-shined wingtips than No-Neck Mareck, with his boss in tow. I nodded hello to him as he escorted the man through our fraternity lounge, describing everything as he went as if he were a White House tour guide. Despite Ed's valiant efforts, the dour, unsmiling man with him was clearly extremely bored. The twosome walked straight toward the trophy case when Ed's eyes caught sight of my beautiful testament to his legacy. His eyes were as big as saucers when his business associate also caught sight of the shining object and strained to read what it said. Ed shifted into immediate panic mode and yelled something like: "Oh my gosh! Look out there, a topless coed!" as he grabbed the man's shoulder and shoved him out of the room toward a window. I am not sure how long Ed stayed with that company, but I did get his message loud and clear as he flashed me the one-fingered salute behind his back as he ushered the man out of the building. I guess people just change?

Typical evening study group session at the Lambda Chi Alpha fraternity house

Meanwhile, national and world affairs were becoming more and more turbulent by the day. The Johnson administration continued to escalate our presence in Vietnam. In a single year from 1965 to 1966, American troop strength more than doubled, from 185,000 to over 385,000. It soon became difficult to remember that our involvement there had at first been generally popular to the man on the street. Support for the war plummeted, especially on college campuses where the institution of the draft would have an ominous, direct, and far-reaching effect. War protests proliferated across the country. Draft card burning, sit-ins, peace rallies, and general civil disobedience were reported daily in the press. Seemingly spontaneous erupting race riots brought the National Guard out in several cities. By then I am sure we began to figure it out: our own tickets for Southeast Asia were already pre-punched. By 1969, over a half-million Americans, including those three unsuspecting 1962 high school graduates, had laid their lives on the line in the jungles of that God-forsaken country.

Back on campus, we had muddled through the hard winter mainly by partying and marking time to graduation only a few weeks away. The Corps was anxiously awaiting our arrival, but we had a few other items to take care of first. Among the most pressing was finding a place to live as newly minted second "looies." The bachelors could just move into the Bachelor Officers Quarters (BOQ) on base, but with wives, we all needed somewhere "out in the ville" close to The Basic School ("TBS") in Quantico. Government-supplied housing was not an option.

All three of us were pretty confident that by signing on with the likes of us, our chosen spouses were geared up to tolerate a lot. That said, we were at least savvy enough to understand that finding suitable housing was imperative if we wanted to preserve the domestic tranquility. With such overwhelming concerns for our spouses' comfort firmly in mind, we launched a mission down to Virginia. I was elected driver by a two-to-one vote, and also got to supply the wheels in the form of my father's battle-hardened VW bug with the door reattached. We set off from Providence bright and early on a Friday morning in May, hoping to complete our mission and be back to Brown early the next week. There was the minor matter of final "finals" and comprehensive exams in our majors yet to be dealt with. As we rolled west and south through Connecticut, there was over a quarter ton of beef crammed into that tiny vehicle. I guess it was a good thing that we weren't leaving the University of Colorado or some other western college for a trip over tall mountains. I doubt that little vehicle could have made it.

We weren't very far along on our journey when the subject of marriage came up. What were we supposed to talk about, Brown football? Jerry and I prattled on about how busy our gals were in making plans for the big event. After a few minutes, I noted that, totally out of character, Charlie was a non-contributor to this stimulating conversation. I decided to ask him about his plans.

A smirk appeared on his face as he explained, "Well you see, Eight ball, Carol and I don't need to bother with that step."

Now this was 1966, and even in those days, plenty of unmarried people cohabitated, but it was still fairly unusual in college. Undaunted, I charged forward and continued my line of questioning. "Well, why not, Chazzz? Are you two going to live in sin?" It was an open secret that they had been living together in an off-campus apartment for a while.

Charlie ignored my rejoinder and remained taciturn. He just looked ahead and smiled. Then it hit me. What an idiot I was. The answer was so obvious. "No kidding!" I finally replied. "But what about the Navy program? You can't be married or you'll be kicked out. What if the major or Ron Benoit find out? Aren't you taking a chance?"

Again, Charlie remained silent with that funny grin on his face. Duh! Again, I slowly caught on. Of course, they knew. The last thing those two Marines would let happen was to lose a Charlie Pigott on a technicality a couple of months before he was about to get his bars anyway. The Corps protects its own. It wasn't the first or last time someone looked the other way when it came to those particular regs. Every once in a while, common sense did prevail in the military.

Finally, I caught myself before I almost blurted out yet another dumb question; why did you get married? I actually figured it out on my own. I glanced over at him, and threw as hard a punch as I could muster in those tight quarters at his shoulder. Now *I* had the big smile. "When is she due, and what names have you picked out?" Jerry hadn't added much to our exchange, but I suspect his pre-trip level of "intel" was higher than mine.

That news was a good way to start the trip. I couldn't wait to tell Joyce, but cell phones would not be invented for another thirty years or so. It would have to wait.

Even though we all had been on the USN payroll with glossy, blue fifty-buck checks magically appearing in our mailboxes each month, we were still three college kids from working-class backgrounds. No one ever had much cash. I don't recall having to wait for either of them while they went to the bank to cash a check before we left Providence. Somehow we'd get along, even though gas had skyrocketed to $.32 per gallon. I do not think we were quite so desperate as to try to sleep in the Bug, but we were certainly open to ways to economize. As things turned out, Jerry led this austerity effort. In fact, it wasn't long before we were rolling down the Connecticut Turnpike, which was a toll road even then. It seemed like there were toll booths every five miles or so that greedily demanded quarters that we didn't have, in order to get that magic green "go" light. Those tolls threatened to blow our trip budget right out of the water, but Jerry rose to the occasion from the backseat.

"Okay, Bob," he began. "You are the driver, and this is almost all on you. Pay attention to me. You too, Charlie."

"Huh?"

"When you approach the next toll booth, slow down about fifteen to twenty feet or so before we reach the basket. Roll down your window and pinch your two fingers together like you have a quarter ready to be tossed into the basket. Are you with me?"

"Sure, Jerry. Do you think I went to the University of Rhode Island?"

"Okay, move up to the toll booth and make like you tossed your coin into the basket but missed. Look angry. That's important, but then take right off. There's probably a car right behind you anyway. The cops at the toll booth don't want to hold up traffic."

"That's great, but what if they come after us? Then what?"

"No problem, Bob. You just explain to them that you missed the basket. There are always lots of stray quarters on the ground around the toll booths. People do miss all the time."

Charlie piped up, "Really?"

"Yep. You'd be surprised."

Sure enough, when we pulled up to the next booth, I faked the toss and then tromped it. No one came after us, despite the loud sounding of alarm bells. As I had started to slow down, Charlie opened his door and discovered that Jerry knew what he was talking about. There were quarters on the pavement everywhere. He scooped up as many as he could, which was usually at least two or three. We actually made a profit going down the turnpike. Jerry's system worked like a charm. Hey, I wonder if that is why he never reimbursed me for gas on the trip?

After routing around the Big Apple via the Tappan Zee Bridge over the Hudson, we fought our way through New Jersey, Delaware, Maryland, and DC. We entered northern Virginia and had most of Saturday to go apartment hunting. We drove down I-95 from the capital about twenty miles and pulled off at Woodbridge, which was about fifteen more miles north of the base in a straight shot down the interstate. Woodbridge seemed like a good place to look and, in a fairly short time, and I decided to lease in the Bayvue Apartments. For some of us, that property would become our first home as a married couple. The units were clean and pretty plain, but, hey, we didn't know any better then. I believe our rent was in the hundred-fifty-dollars-per-month range, which seems cheap, but was still barely affordable on a second lieutenant's salary. Today, the comparable units start at around a grand or even higher. By the way, I think I remember actually looking inside our apartment-to-be before signing the lease, but I am really not sure I went to that extreme. The place was handy to Route 1 and the interstate. We could be at TBS in half an hour. Mission accomplished. Let's go grab a beer.

The way our TBS schedule would be structured, we were going to be out there most of the time anyway. How about 0700 to 1900? We couldn't expect to spend a lot of time lounging around at home. Jerry and Charlie, apparently decided that Bayvue was too pricey for their blood. They found less expensive places in other complexes further down the freeway closer to Quantico. I think the real reason they didn't rent at Bayvue was because after experiencing my driving for some seven hundred miles from Providence, they did not look forward to the prospect of carpooling with me to work. Thinking about that trip today, it is fascinating that three irresponsible male college boys could be trusted by their soon-to-be spouses to pick out a place to live strictly on their own call. When Joyce eventually saw our apartment, she was tickled and said it was "cute." I don't think she even complained about counter and cabinet space. Today, I cannot make a decision where to hang a flyswatter without receiving detailed instruction and guidance. So much for the age of instant information.

Marital arrangements notwithstanding, during our long haul back and forth from Virginia, we did discuss a lot of stuff, most of which pertained to the USMC of all things. As I have described I was fully on board, gung ho, or whatever term is best applied, but I had been later to the party than Jerry and Charlie. Jerry had wanted to fly jets from his high school days and hoped to do it with his buddy, Gene Mares, back in New York.

Charlie seemed to see things a little bit differently. He was determined to measure up and prove that he could succeed in the toughest circumstances possible. If he ever had second thoughts, I never saw any hint of them. During this trip, he said he was anxious not only to get into the Corps, but also to get to Vietnam where the action was. While that attitude was certainly not unusual among young men during wartime back then and even now, I had to ask him why he was so eager to put himself in harm's way. On cue, Charlie fired right back at me. I will never forget his response; "I want to go because the true test of a man is in combat." I had heard him repeat those words on several occasions. I have no doubt that he truly believed that statement.

In many ways, that house-hunting trip to Virginia in the spring of 1966 marked the start of a new chapter in the lives of three young guys, all literally in the same boat. We were full of life and anxious to move on from college into the real world. We were comfortable with our families and the direction of our livelihoods in the USMC. It was an exciting time, even with the shadow of the contentious Vietnam War hanging over our heads. We shared a mutual disdain for those who felt that our country was dead wrong for being caught up in a civil war in Southeast Asia. Even if we did not absolutely buy everything we were fed from those on high about the conflict, we were determined to do our sworn duty for our country. We could sort out the bigger issues, pros and cons, after we got home. We resolutely marched off to war as ordered. I was the only one to come home. I will never quite understand why if two of us had to perish that I was the incredibly lucky one to live out a full life.

CHAPTER 24

I Got Married Twice That Week

My mother always said that her happiest time in her life was the final year of high school. She certainly had a point; life in high school was truly much simpler than it promised to be in the years that followed. Responsibilities were non-existent, friends were sincere, and naivety about the real world was comforting. While I don't necessarily agree with her, the idea is well taken. We were now on the precipice of leaving the coziness of the university, where, like it or not, we had been thoroughly programed for the past four years. Certainly, we had encountered rigorous and demanding courses, agonized over grades and GPAs, and struggled with relationships, especially with the opposite sex. In reality, however, the past four years would pale compared to what lay ahead. In fact, we were impatient to get on with our lives. We were as ready as we would ever be. Bring it on.

It would be too simple, I suppose, for Brown University to have "graduation" exercises. No, at Brown, we have "commencement," which is crammed full of pageantry and tradition. The Van Wickle Gates are opened only two times each year, and commencement is one of them. A procession including the senior class and various other dignitaries, politicians, and big wigs pass through and gathers down College Hill at the old First Baptist Meeting House for a brief ceremony. It is very significant to note that our ritual in the meeting house included both a *prayer* and *the national anthem*. I wonder if those items continue to appear on the programs today. I suspect not. It is there that the designated senior class orators deliver their speeches.

The entire group then marches back up the Hill to the College Green for the actual conferring of degrees. In our case, the 198th Commencement took place on Monday, June 6, 1966, at 11:00 a.m.—excuse me—1100 hours. Brown does get a few points right there. Unlike almost everywhere else, there is no famous and noteworthy invited speaker to tell us to "go forth and follow your dreams." There were a few honorary degrees given out. Leonard Bernstein was the only one of any significance that I recall in 1966. As compared to most august institutions of higher learning, the Brown spectacle is relatively brief and tolerable.

President Barnaby Keeney presided at our graduation, er, commencement as one of his last official acts. Of the total of 1,245 degrees conferred, there were 198 to Pembroke and 568 to Brown seniors. Incidentally, I am amused to note that "Carol Crockett Pigott" was listed on the Pembroke list. I hope Major Whelan didn't see that. Somehow, they missed Jerry, Charlie, and me on the summa, magna, and cum laude lists, although I did note that Clark Hopson, one of our "animal house" Lambda Chi brothers, did appear on the cum laude list. As I recall, he was very bright and became a physician, even though he was not very good at hall hockey.

The presentation of baccalaureate diplomas was immediately followed by Administration of Oath and Awarding of Commissions. Here is another area where the Brown higher ups found a way to make the ceremony shorter in the years after we left. No ROTC, no wasted time in June for commissioning.

We were decked out in our dress white uniforms. I don't remember any jeers or comments from the crowd, but I would not have been surprised if there were some. The most virulent and hostile distaste for all things military at Brown was yet to come, but the seeds of discontent were fomenting at the time we graduated. Looking back at a *Providence Evening Bulletin* article on our commencement, I discovered something that had escaped me all these years. If the piece is accurate, the oath of commission was administered to all ROTC Marine, Navy, and Air Force together by *Air Force* Brigadier General Wright J. Sherrod from Otis Air Force Base on Cape Cod. Holy cow! Was that legal? An Air "Farce" guy swore us in. Maybe we were never really in the Corps. Take it away, junior birdmen! Shudder the thought.

On a side note, in perusing the 6-6-66 *Evening Bulletin*, I noticed that the biggest news of the day was the "Safe Bull's Eye Landing of the Gemini Spaceship." For one day at least, NASA had bumped RVN from the headlines. There were ads for a "chiffon float, curvy crepe skimmer for divine dinner and dancing, only $22.95," and special weekend rates including breakfast at the Commodore Hotel in New York for $5.75 per night per person. There it is, dramatic proof that things weren't so bad out there in the real world as we prepared to enter it.

6/6/66 - Commencement and Commissioning.
One marriage down and one yet to go.

The record shows that twenty-nine NROTC and four AFROTC commissions were awarded during the ceremony. There were seven new USMC second lieutenants. Besides Jerry, Charlie, and myself, Tom Drummond, Dave Taylor, Billy Peters, and Paul Ryan became sworn officers in the Corps. Missing from this ceremony was Paul Kelly, who had taken additional courses. He officially graduated and was commissioned later. Jeff Hayes was no longer a midshipman, but did also subsequently earn his degree. While I had forgotten about the Air Force Brigadier General, I have always remembered who pinned my gold bars on—my beautiful fiancée, with our own ceremony only five days away. In fact, on June 11, the knot was permanently tied at the Brightwood Christian Church in Bethel Park, Pennsylvania. Our best man was my high school chum, Harry Potter. Harry must have cast a spell on us because it has been a storybook romance ever since.

It is appropriate, I think, at this point to make a few comments about the institution from which I had just graduated. I thoroughly enjoyed my time there and met some of the most wonderful people imaginable. Those folks and Brown University have continued to influence my life to this day. The academics were challenging, but not overwhelming, and the university admirably was sincere in helping anyone who reached out for help. Brown was an exciting place that exuded a magnetic field that drew students from all over the country. It has always prided itself on its diversity, and even then on a de facto, non-proactive basis, it always had a wide variety of students from all backgrounds and beliefs. In our day, it was not a contrived diversity.

Brown also, during those days, was decidedly undergraduate oriented. We were the primary focus of the entire institution. The graduate programs were very limited and not necessarily recognized as being world-class. The corporation has certainly found it necessary in order to compete in today's academic environment to greatly upgrade the Brown master's, doctoral, and beyond programs. Such refocusing has to come, to some extent, at the expense of the undergraduate student.

From the day I arrived on campus to this moment, I have never regarded Brown University as "warm and fuzzy." I view it as an aggregate of extremely bright individuals who are free to express their overwhelmingly liberal ideas in whatever direction they choose, irrespective of traditional societal norms or expectations. "Anything goes for me" seems infused in the fabric of the place. Brown champions individual thought and always has, which is by no means a bad thing.

Even in my day, shortly after I graduated, a brilliant undergraduate and individualist, Ira Magaziner, attempted to totally reform the curriculum into a full "pass-fail" configuration. In the purest sense, that sounds great. Even I could pursue courses that I was interested in but was fearful of getting a low grade. Bring on nuclear engineering.

As Brown discovered, however, such utopian ideas don't always work out so well in practice. Suddenly, Brown graduates could not get into more traditional advanced degree programs that required minimal GPA achievement standards. Revisions had to be made. Even Brown University, the shining beacon of individualism, must function within the context of a much larger society.

Somehow, however, Brown University has been quite content to look down with disfavor upon a key component of our society. I have personally found the blatant negative regard toward our military over the last several decades to be reprehensible. In fairness, Brown today has established an office of military affairs and gives lip service to supporting students who choose to serve. Frankly, it turns my stomach that Brown students have to go to Providence College or Holy Cross in Worcester, Massachusetts for ROTC. The elimination of the ROTC programs at Brown in the 1970s to me was a self-serving act of selfishness instigated by those students and faculty who felt personally threatened. Perhaps *they* could have been called to serve. It has never made any sense to me that one of the most liberal bastions of self-determination extant foreclosed on certain avenues and programs that *some* students would have chosen to pursue. In other words, everything goes, so long as they like it.

Many of those thirty or so students who graduated and were commissioned with me, as well as others who were associated with the expelled ROTC programs, served this country with incredible distinction. I doubt very much that many of us could have even attended Brown without the ROTC programs. In exchange for the assistance we received to attend one of the world's most outstanding places of higher education, we unselfishly agreed to uphold our sworn obligations to perform our duty. While Brown students were burning draft cards and faculty members were openly displaying their jealousy of the Professor of Naval Science, those Brown men and women were winning Navy Crosses, Bronze Stars, and numerous other awards for gallantry and valor, all in an effort to maintain the freedom that everyone cherishes. "Great personal sacrifice" does not begin to describe these brave men. At least three Brown alumni paid the ultimate price without even the courtesy of a perfunctory thank you. Even if those gallant souls had come home, as I did, it wouldn't have mattered; they still would have been rejects on College Hill. Brown's blind spot in this regard shall trouble me for all my remaining days.

CHAPTER 25

The Basic School

THE CLANKING OF SLAMMED METAL locker doors, scuffling of boots on polished floors, and clipped bits of conversation echoed through the building early on that sticky Monday morning in July. It was 1966, and our country was continuing to become more and more mired in a shooting war in Southeast Asia. The next class of one hundred fifty new second lieutenants scrambled to stow their gear and fall out for their initial formation as a company at The Basic School located on the United States Marine Corps base at Quantico in northern Virginia. It was truly the first day of the rest of our lives. In fact, some of us, tragically, would not see his next birthday.

The dawn was breaking as groups of young men clad in standard USMC green utilities with black combat boots streamed out of the building onto the parade deck below, where we milled and shifted until everyone found his alphabetically designated proper platoon, squad, fire team, and spot. The bachelors among us had come over from the BOQ on the base, but the married men had to drive in from apartments they'd secured in scattered towns and villages outside the main gate. After rising at o'dark thirty, jumping into our uniforms for really the first time, hastily pecking our respective brand-new wife on the cheek, we floored it down I-95, praying the Virginia state troopers were still on coffee break. Once we arrived, we bolted into the building, crammed our equipment into our assigned lockers, and hustled out to the first real USMC activity. Perish the thought that anyone might be late.

At precisely 0730 on the 5th of July, 1966, a stentorian: "Atten-hut!" bellowed out from somewhere up front. Reacting as a single unit, the mass of young officerhood snapped erect and transfixed its collective gaze straight ahead. The commanding officer, a major, emerged smartly from one side and executed squared turns as he moved directly to the front and center, where he stood facing the stiffened group. The company was divided into four platoons, A through D, with some forty-four men each, including an assigned regular Marine platoon leader from the TBS staff who already had taken position directly in front of his respective charges.

The CO paused and took his time to drink in his new company, which he was seeing for the first time. Finally, after what seemed an interminable period, he ordered: "At ease!" which caused us to physically uncoil in unison from the ramrod-straight stance by spreading our legs to shoulder width and clasping our hands behind our backs. We were already ahead of OCS, where we were kept at attention for what seemed like forever. At that point, no one was truly "at ease"; a mere posture change did little to ease our concern for what lay ahead. We accorded rapt attention to our new leader, who was about to tell us just what was in store over the next several months that would magically transform us from irresponsible college students to real Marines and leaders of men.

"Welcome to the United States Marine Corps and The Basic School at Quantico, Virginia," he burst forth in a forceful and fervent, no-bs tone that indisputably established his command bearing. "You are now members of the most elite fighting force in the history of the world. You are privileged to be standing here today. It will be our job over the next several weeks to make sure you belong here. The hours will be long. We officially work five and a half days a week but expect more. You will start before first light in the morning and will not finish until long after sunset each evening. You will be challenged, tested, measured, pushed, and prodded. You will not be urged, encouraged, babied, or coddled. It will be up to you to sink or swim. We have the finest programs and facilities anywhere. You will be exposed to every weapon in our arsenal. You will attend classes given by our excellent staff of instructors. You will learn history, tactics, conducting small unit warfare, and much more. There will be plenty of time in the field with forced marches, weapons training, and tactical exercises. You will be rated on three areas: physical readiness, classroom work, and leadership. You must seek to excel in all three. All are important. We have no room for slackers or unmotivated individuals. When you are through here you must be ready to assume the deadly serious job of leading a rifle platoon into combat. If we think you are not, then perhaps you should consider the Air Force."

"Now I want each and every one of you to listen to me very closely. What I am about to say is extremely important. Our mission here is critical. We are in the middle of a conflict in the Republic of Vietnam. The course you are about to go through has been compressed and accelerated to process qualified platoon leaders through as rapidly as possible. You will accomplish in four and a half months what used to take six. There is no time to waste. We are duty bound to reach our objectives. There is one and only one way that you can truly succeed in this man's United States Marine Corps. The Corps must come first in every aspect of your life. There is no compromising that point. I know most of you have families back home, and that many of you have brand-new wives. These people must now come second to the Corps. In the months and years ahead, you will be put into life-and-death situations that call for instant action. There can be no wavering or hesitation; you must be prepared to make the best decision in the interests of your fellow Marines. The fact that you are standing here today means you are totally dedicated to serving your country as a United States Marine. There are no higher priorities. I hope I have made myself clear." (This portion of the opening instruction may be loosely translated to: "*If the Marine Corps wanted you to have a wife, they would have issued you one.*")

"Each of you has been assigned to a platoon, which will be led by a regular Marine staff instructor. Pay attention to them, work hard, and you should do well over the next several weeks. I wish you good luck, and look forward to congratulating you on successfully completing the TBS course and embarking on your orders to the Fleet Marine Force. Good luck. Semper fi, gentlemen. Platoon leaders, you are in command of your men."

Another "Atten-hut" was followed by the company coming to attention. The commander smartly pivoted and strutted off. We had been assigned to platoons alphabetically. I was in First Platoon, Charlie was in Third Platoon, and Mr. Zimmer, of course, was in Fourth Platoon. The First Platoon was greeted by Captain Roger Lamphear, who in a very roundabout way resembled Barney Fife. The captain was under six feet, thin, and had a ruddy complexion. His Adams apple tended to flip up and down when he talked. Standing before us, he did not spontaneously convey by his stature and demeanor an overwhelming sense of command presence or bearing. What he may have lacked in appearance, however, he more than made up for in the vigor of his personality. It was clear that he had a job to do: turn out some forty or so Marine officers in just a few months. He was determined to do it without a lot of horsing around or grab-ass. At all times he strived to remain in control and aloof. Clearly, it was not his intent to be buddy-buddy with the troops. Very early on, he drew the boundaries between us. He was in charge, and we were to do perfectly what he said, when he said it. I suppose that relationship was more than fair and what we had been expecting. After a brief reiteration of the CO's remarks we were off and double-timing to our first class.

Life at TBS for us brand-new second "johns" turned out to be very similar to OCS the previous summer, although there were, of course, many differences. We were now commissioned officers, and the staff running the program really did not want us to wash out. The Corps had a crying need for us out in the FMF ("Fleet Marine Force") as soon as possible. Vietnam was escalating like crazy. Scant as it seemed at times, we were accorded more respect from Captain Lamphear and the TBS staff than had been the case with the drill instructors the previous summer. While tight discipline and attention to detail were still important, there was very little harassment just for harassment's sake. We were on a power curve to learn. There wasn't a lot of time for inane bull just for the sake of keeping us off guard. We continued to be herded around from place to place by double timing or sometimes in the USMC's own special kind of conveyance—the cattle car. These wonderful vehicles were nothing more than 18-wheeler trailers pulled by truck cabs. There were doors in the center where we scrambled in to hard wooden benches with gray iron pipe railings. The interior floors sloped about 30 degrees. They were uncomfortable as hell, but were actually a very welcome sight after a long forced march or late field exercise.

We were issued a published schedule about one week ahead, which told us the type, time, and location of all activities. There was a lot of outdoor classroom instruction with us sitting on bleachers. Much of the weapons training was done using this format. I remember one particular class on survival tactics where a squared-away, recruiting poster-looking gunnery sergeant stood before the group explaining how to find water and things to eat in the wild. All the time he was stroking and petting a pretty white bunny with big brown eyes that nuzzled his hand while he talked. As he droned on about how to get along on your own, a buzz and whispering started through the crowd of us rough-and-tough second lieutenants. "You don't suppose he's going to...?. No, he wouldn't do that, would he? I sure hope not." Of course, he would, and he did. He held up that little wiggling and squirming rabbit for all to see and gave it one hard karate chop. The audience was aghast and shaken. That poor little defenseless bunny! It didn't help matters when the sergeant skinned it, stuck his hand in the skin, and held it up like Bugs Bunny. "What's up, Doc?" Marines?

In addition to "bunnycide," the program at TBS was designed to expose us to every weapon in the Marine Corps arsenal. We were able to fire most of them. We threw live grenades and shouted "fire in the hole!" in our toughest voices. Most of us remembered to duck. We fired recoilless rifles and various artillery pieces, including the .55 mm howitzer. We used grenade launchers and rifle grenades that gave a healthy kick and, ironically, have become such a favorite weapon in the current age of paramilitary and terrorist operations. There were 3.5-inch rocket launchers, which looked something like the old bazookas. We were instructed how to use 81 mm mortars. We did not fire the brand-new M16 rifles, which had not quite been introduced as yet and then created so much controversy because they jammed so often in combat. We got to participate in live fire exercises where we crawled under barbed wire with real bullets zinging over our heads. I don't think you could have raised up if you wanted to. Just the same, most of us finished that event having eaten quite a bit of delicious TBS mud.

Of all the weapons, perhaps my least favorite was the M60 machine gun. This little baby was designed to be carried in a rifle platoon. It could put out something like 500 to 600 rounds per minute and weighed almost 24 pounds. It was heavy to lug around, but most grunts were very happy to have it when things got hot in combat. It was fun to fire but, as I discovered, was a bit temperamental when it came to keeping it clean. We fired the M60 on the range one afternoon and then were hauled back to TBS in our cattle cars. It was probably only about 1830 or so—not too bad a time to call it a day. All we had to do was clean up our machine guns, turn them in, and head home. Should take about half an hour tops. Well, maybe not.

That day, I had fired with Kent Wilson, who was actually a lawyer headed for the judge advocate's office after he finished the course. Kent, hardly the typical Marine stereotype, was an affable sort, and we got along just fine on the range. Unfortunately, neither of us turned out to be very proficient in breaking down and cleaning the M60. Captain Lamphear was the inspector and gatekeeper of those who could go home. He alone determined if your weapon was clean *enough* or not. We must have hauled that damn thing back to him ten times. He always came up with some black carbon grease we missed. Meanwhile, the sun had set in the west. It was approaching 2200. We had been there for hours, but finally were dead sure we finally had the thing spotless. The captain sat there with a disgusted and languid look in his eyes as he ran his hands all over the piece. I held my breath. Everything looked perfect. Then he took his little skinny pinky and inserted it deep into the breach. He wiggled it once, pulled it out, and held up his black little digit. Kent and I were crestfallen. Both of us had pinkies that were too fat to fit into the breach. Somehow, we finally staggered out of there. Joyce greeted me when I arrived home at midnight. The M60 was a killer weapon, all right.

We also spent time on both the pistol range with the .45s and the rifle range with the M-14s. This time we fired the ranges for a score and earned shiny badges. Depending on your total, you were either an expert, sharpshooter, or marksman, so long as you met the minimum score to qualify. Somehow, I fired expert in both. We were required to requalify every year, and I never did as well again.

Marines stick together, and we look out for each other. In those days you had your buddies working in the rifle range butts under the targets. A shooter would fire his ten rounds from a certain yard line. The guys in the butts would crank down the target and insert markers in the holes where each shot hit the paper. A miss rated a wave of Maggie's drawers—and zero points, by the way. If a man was actually firing for score to qualify, the butt's crew would usually keep score as he progressed. If the guy needed a few points to qualify, the butts guys were usually more than accommodating. Just try and hit the target at 500 yards with your elevation and wind clicks still set for 300.

They had constructed a faux Hollywood-like Vietnamese village at TBS back in the woods. We ran several instructive team drills on how to approach and clear buildings and rooms. There was lots of PT, especially long runs in platoon formation along the roads around the base. We had forced marches over the infamous "hill trail." It was the middle of summer in Virginia and pretty damn hot, but they were trying to train and condition us, not kill us. We made regular trips to the O course, which I had down pretty well by then. I was hardly a squirrel scrambling up the rope, but I could make it every time. I was up to about five chin-ups, a personal record. We also tried the "confidence course," which was supposed to build you up after you conquered the difficult obstacles. I had no trouble getting up and down high cargo nets tied between two tall pine trees. The ladder, though, was another question. Two very tall telephone poles, perhaps 50 feet high, were positioned parallel to each other about fifteen feet apart. Logs of various diameters were fixed horizontally at differing gaps all the way up. The idea was to go up one side and down the other. I made it about halfway up. The gap to the next log was almost five feet. A monkey, I am not. It was definitely easier for a tall, agile person.

I recall watching Charlie on that one. He was partway up and stayed there for a long time, not wanting to give up. He was determined to make it, and I am sure he did. One of our NROTC summer cruise contemporaries from Cornell, Bruce Mansdorf, happened to be on the ladder with Charlie. While Bruce was a good athlete and lacrosse player, he was considerably shorter than Charlie. With the distance between the horizontal logs ranging from two to up to five feet or so, being tall was a definite advantage on that obstacle. Bruce recounts how difficult it was for him to climb between logs set so far apart while being thirty feet or so in the air. Bruce was all set to throw in the towel when the big guy next to him began to encourage him to keep at it. Charlie wouldn't let him quit. Bruce credits Charlie's support for making it that day. Charlie was never reluctant to lend a hand to a friend. As for me, I am glad we only ran that course once, or my confidence really would have been shaken.

It was too late for the Corps to recruit us, but even after signing up it can be gratifying to know that you have truly associated yourself with the very best. On a summer Friday evening, B Company was assembled and transported into Washington, DC, proper. I believe we actually traveled in real busses and not cattle cars, which seemed to be reserved for intra-base movements. Our destination that evening was the Marine Corps Barracks at Eighth and I streets in the nation's capital. The facility, which was built in 1801, is on the National Register of Historic places and is the ceremonial home of the Corps. The commandant resides there, as well as the Marine Band, Drum and Bugle Corps, and Silent Drill Team. We were on hand to watch the Sunset Parade, which is as impressive a display of pomp and ceremony as I can imagine. The performance is awe inspiring, with precision marching of the band members and buglers. The show stopper is the Silent Drill Team, which moves up and down the parade deck without ever shouting a command while performing intricate and exact formations, including exchanging rifles with affixed bare bayonets. Anyone who has ever worn a Marine uniform has to be immensely proud to witness that event. Anyone visiting Washington should try to schedule time to see this spectacle. TBS boredom and frustration were set aside for a while that night. To a man, we were all ready to take on whatever poor unfortunate enemy crossed our path.

The next Monday we were back to reality with the condensed training program. One of my favorite events was hand-to-hand combat using pugil sticks, which looks really rough and tough but you are so well protected that chances of an injury are minimal. We wore helmets and were on an elevated platform. The idea was to knock the other guy off before he did the same to you. The pugil sticks were lightweight pipes about five feet long that had round cushioned padding on either end. It was fun to let the other guy have it. We studied small unit tactics in the classroom, weapons, nomenclature, some history, USMC organization, compass reading, and many other topics, all aimed at preparing us to be rifle platoon commanders at the end of the course. There was also a section on the "Technique of Military Instruction," which should have had a section that taught us how to be staccato, factual, monotone, and boring, since many instructors seemed to possess those qualities. I had to prepare a presentation, including charts, and teach an actual class on the use of the claymore mines. Not only did I learn about the weapon, but it was also good to stand on your feet and address a group. It was nice to have an audience that had to choose listening to me or getting thrown into the brig. At that, some of them might have chosen bars over Bob. For our grand finale at TBS, we ran an overnight exercise, "war," against enemy aggressors with judges. I remember being exhausted after it was over but not much else. I guess we won.

CHAPTER 26

Dear Friends Say Good Bye

THE OFFICIAL RIFLE PLATOON LEADER training we received that summer and fall of 1966 demanded a high percentage of our waking hours, but the interpersonal relationships we enjoyed during those few months meant so much more to us than all the rote instruction and formal field exercises that were thrown at us. For the very first time in our lives, we found ourselves truly on our own. Like it or not, we had finally severed ties with our childhood. Many of us were also adjusting to the rigors of married life, which is no mean feat in itself. On top of all else, the proverbial "elephant in the room" was lurking: we were all going off to war in the immediate future. We were not a bunch of Citibank trainees who would be assigned to bank audit departments when the training was over. The ache of separation aside, while it was unspoken, everyone knew that very likely, some of us would never return. We all scrutinized the daily military newspaper, *Stars and Stripes*, for the names of RVN casualties. Some days there were just a few. On others there were startling numbers of forty or fifty. By the end of TBS we began to recognize some of the KIA Marines we knew, some of whom had been only a class or two ahead of us at TBS. A few months earlier, they'd been living, breathing trainees right here, just like us. Now they were gone. We tried to keep that newspaper away from our wives.

Despite these collateral concerns waiting in the background, I don't recall being overly concerned or worried about the future. Looking back, I still regard that six-month period as one of the most memorable, exciting, and gratifying times in my life.

Joyce and I were thrown together with some of the most wonderful friends we would ever encounter. The relationships we made during those few months have lasted a lifetime, even without much contact through the years. We all shared a bond that can never be broken. Be it bitching about the checkers at the base PX, our long hours, always being broke, the idiots who were running our program, flat tires, noisy neighbors, and a hundred other things, we were all in it together. We knew time was precious, and tried to socialize as much as we could. We shared meals, visited each other's apartments, car pooled, and picnicked whenever we could.

Since several of us lived in Woodbridge and kept the same long hours at TBS, carpooling together back and forth to Quantico seemed to make good sense. I guess I should have had some trepidations about that arrangement, but, then again, at that time I was a tough Marine who feared nothing. Looking back now, I should have thought twice about risking life and limb with a far left-coaster from Oregon who drove a 1966 Pontiac Tempest that his wife had affectionately named "Smedley," after one to the Corp's most revered legendary generals.

We were headed home one evening along the old Shirley Highway that was part of Route 1 with John Metschan at the wheel of Trudie's precious Smedley. After a long day of Roger Lamphear's rantings, none of the three of us on board were on full or even partial alert, including the driver.

That area of Virginia has rolling hills, and the four-lane, full-access, limited-sight highway was jammed with businesses, side streets, and traffic lights, which tended to pop up when you least expected them. Not far from home, John had Smedley purring like a kitten with his foot down pretty heavy. Normally that wasn't much of a problem because he and Smedley had developed a unique symbiotic understanding with each other over the miles. Unfortunately, however, in this case, as we topped the crest of a hill, a traffic light suddenly appeared just a few yards away, which was trouble enough. To complicate matters, we were barreling toward a car just ahead of us in our lane signaling for a left turn. Traffic clogged the right lane. Sitting next to John, I awoke from a stupor just in time to take in the oncoming disaster and ram my combat boot repeatedly against the floorboards to apply a non-existent brake pedal.

I guess I should not have worried. The "Scmed-Met" team had gotten us into that mess, and they would get us out. With zero other options, John yanked the wheel to the left and entered the southbound lane, directly in the path of oncoming traffic. Somehow, we flew past the left turner, who thankfully must have been frozen in fear. He then swerved back to the right, narrowly missing a head-on collision with traffic headed south. John had slowed down considerably when I dared open my eyes. I think I was able to stammer a "Holy Shit" at that point. John offered only a weak smile.

I turned and looked at Charlie in the back seat. "Charlie, did you see that? What we just did?"

His eyebrows lifted slightly as he slowly yawned, "Sure. I saw it. So what? Hurry up and get home. I'm hungry."

Sunday was the only day we truly had for our wives and ourselves. Virginia is a beautiful place, especially along the western border in the Shenandoah Valley and the Blue Ridge Mountains. On a few very special occasions, a group of us, including Charlie and Carol, John and Trudie Metschan, Ed and Sandy Eloe, Al and Darlene Buescher, Ray and Nancy Daly, Tom and Cathy Gleason, Bruce Mansdorf, John Holderness, and a few others, would load up our cars and drive out through Front Royal and up on to the Blue Ridge Parkway that over looked the Shenandoah

Valley, where we would pick a picturesque spot for a picnic. One of the guys who attended those picnics recalled our putting together detail "op orders" in the best USMC tradition. Paragraph 4.2, a. iii. "Pigott, you are assigned the beer." That kind of stuff.

Unfortunately, Jerry and Elaine, who lived some miles away, weren't able to join us on these outings. I am certain, however, that this period was also a time for them of enjoying interaction with fellow TBS classmates and their wives. Tom Thompson related an amusing story about playing bridge with Elaine. The Thompsons were Midwesterners who'd had little contact at that time with folks from back East. When Elaine bid "four hots," they had no idea what she was talking about. It took a while for them to adjust to the Yankee accent, although, ironically, they ended up settling in Vermont, where they have spent the last 45 years. Tom didn't mention whether or not they now bid "hots" or "hearts" at the bridge table.

Maybe it was the circumstances, our companions, or maybe even the alcohol, but I remember that area of western Virginia as one of the most beautiful places on earth. The gorgeous stands of tall hardwoods, rocky meadows, lush greenery everywhere, and striking distant mountain vistas were breathtaking. Fall was not that far away, and the hint of chill in the air was a delightful contrast to the heat and humidity back on the lowlands around Quantico. We grilled hot dogs and hamburgers, quaffed beer, and took short hikes around that fanciful place. We told jokes, played stupid games, commiserated, and just reveled in each other's company. It was the perfect getaway and respite from the demands the USMC put on us for the rest of the week.

A big event occurred in Charlie and Carol's lives very early during our Basic School stay with the arrival of their daughter, Stacy. Charlie was, of course, a beaming, proud papa. I received a welcome cigar. Stacy was on hand at my 22nd birthday party at our apartment on November 2. Carol, Charlie, Joyce, and little Stacy all sang happy birthday to me.

That night, Charlie and I talked a lot about what our next assignments might be and where we'd end up. With our TBS time running down, all of a sudden, we began to discover that life in the Corps consisted of a little more than a dawn-to-dusk, never-ending training regimen. Social obligations began to pop up on our schedule, starting with the Marine Corps Ball on November 5. It goes without saying that we second lieutenants looked really sharp in our dress blues, but our attire was drab compared to our gorgeous and stunning wives in their formal long dresses. Up to that point, military life wasn't so tough.

I have one special recollection of that evening at the Officer's Club where the ball was held. We had become good friends with Ray and Nancy Daley. Ray was a terrific person, a fellow New Englander from New Hampshire, and a Naval Academy grad. Nancy was a tiny sweetheart whose bemused outlook provided a perfect complement to her husband's very proper military demeanor. That evening, Nancy capped off her attire at the ball with a tiara of mysterious, unknown origins, which immediately became the target of all our good humor. At some point during the evening, Joyce and I were dancing, when one edge of an overhead net holding balloons came loose from the ceiling. Poor Nancy happened to be under it at the time and unfortunately got her fancy headpiece snarled in the webbing. As luck would have it, just at that moment, some half-tanked major waltzed by and began to drag the net across the floor. Had it not been for my quick action to rescue the fallen princess, there is no telling what might have happened. As it was, the major was very unamused, the jerk.

To an outsider, it might be easy to assume that our last few weeks at the training command were overshadowed by the ominous assignments all of us knew lay just ahead. That situation was simply not the case, and I do not want to leave the impression that those days were melancholy or doleful. The overwhelming majority of us were optimistic, bright-eyed, and eager to get on with our lives. It was a thrilling time to be alive and to have so many close friends. We were universally cheerful and, if anything, saw the anticipated Westpac tour as an exciting challenge and temporary delay in the important business of raising a family. Still, when the actual news came down, the stark reality of it all was disconcerting to some, especially the wives.

One of the very special dates every year on the calendar is November 10, which is the Marine Corps' birthday. Tradition holds that Marines get together to hold a Mess Night on that date to honor and respect those who have gone before them. Everyone wears his ribbons, medals, and finest dress blues, and gathers to enjoy a meal together. There are many, many toasts to many, many people. Alcohol flows very freely and big, ugly, foul-smelling cigars are a must to achieve the proper ambiance. Our Mess Night at TBS was a bit unique in that the head man himself, Commandant of the Marine Corps Lieutenant General Len Chapman, attended in person. His presence, I suspect, was due to the fact that his son, Walt, was a member of our Basic School class. He was, in fact, in my squad.

Having the commandant on hand was a special treat, although it didn't seem to tone down the activities very much. I would hate to think what the average breathalyzer score we would have blown that night as a group would have been. In any event, in his remarks, General Chapman let it be known, and only confirmed what we all already knew anyway. "After you complete your training at TBS, sooner or later, every man in this room is headed for Westpac and Southeast Asia." I'll drink to that, and I did, several times. No big deal; we had not been expecting anything else. We felt we were prepared and, in fact, it would have been difficult to find anyone in our class who, given the chance, would not have volunteered to go. General Chapman's comments merely capped off what was a wonderful and memorable evening.

When I finally staggered home sometime in the wee hours of the next morning and somehow entered the right apartment, my marital sensitivities were clearly blunted by my condition. Thrilled to see my beautiful new bride of five months sitting up in bed, I couldn't wait to blurt out the joyous news that General Chapman had given us. Despite my haze, almost immediately I realized what an idiot I had been. She looked at me and tears welled in her gorgeous eyes. After giving me a brave half-smile and hug, she collapsed on her pillow. I will always remember lying there next to her listening as she sobbed herself to sleep. It is one thing to assume, but quite another to know. Women are funny that way.

Well, it was time to decide just where in this man's USMC you wanted to work. Please understand that by matriculating through TBS, we all had earned the Military Occupational Specialty (MOS) of 0302, which was infantry, rifle platoon commander, and grunt. In addition, we now had an opportunity to choose another MOS specialty, if we so desired. In the Corps, of course, the dream job of every young, brand-new second lieutenant just out of Basic school is supposed to be infantry, rifle platoon commander. I was not so sure, though, that that job was exactly what I wanted as a first choice. Other possibilities were flight, motor transport, artillery, supply, communications, and armor. I had thought a lot about flight, which Jerry and Charlie chose right away. As I mentioned before, flying seemed to be a few seconds of panic on either end of hours of boredom. I just was not that thrilled by flying. Another factor was that according to the flight school pecking order, jets were at the top, and helicopters at the bottom. The need for chopper pilots was highest, for a good reason. Your chance of choppers seemed to be much better than jets or other fixed-wing. So, going to flight school during those times for most meant flying helicopters. Also, even after becoming a pilot, there was a good chance you would serve some time hiking out in the boonies with a grunt company as the forward observer on the ground assisting them to call in air strikes. That didn't seem like too much fun. After thoroughly considering all my options, the only other

MOS that seemed interesting was supply and logistics, which is what I ended up choosing and getting. In some ways, I suppose, it is reasonable to assume that decision may well have saved my life.

Joyce and I on TBS graduation day in Novmber 1966. Finally, I must admit it. I joined for the uniform. I am pretty snazzy in my dress blues, don't you think?

By Thanksgiving Day 1966, TBS was history. We were all certified trained killers. Orders had been issued. I was on my way to supply school at Montfort Point at Camp Lejeune in Jacksonville, North Carolina. Charlie, Jerry, Ray Daley, Dave Taylor, and a bunch of others had gotten flight school and would be headed to Pensacola, when the next class at flight school class was formed. Al Buescher would stay a grunt, John Metschan would also get supply, and Tom Gleason got motor T.

After the formal TBS graduation ceremony in our spiffy white uniforms, as is the case with any graduation, we spent a little time afterward milling around, taking pictures, and saying good-byes. We shook hands and gave each other mock salutes. We were all anxious to get moving and head to the points of the compass for leave time before reporting to our next duty stations. Life was exciting. We now had some time under our belts as real Marines. We weren't "salty," as the saying goes, but we sure sneered at the next class of fresh meat that had arrived at TBS.

We promised to keep in touch, fully well realizing that, other than in chance meetings, what that really meant is we hoped the wives would keep in touch. Those were still letter-writing, paper-and-pen days. We were all off to new, great adventures. In fact, we were probably much more worried about traffic around the Washington beltway as we drove north that day than any inkling of ominous foreboding about our futures. None of us gave such things any thought whatsoever as we moved around shaking hands and wishing each other well. Unfortunately those few, unremarkable, quickly passed hale and hearty see ya laters that morning were the last moments I would ever see Jerry, Charlie, Ray Daley, and some others alive.

CHAPTER 27

Da Nang, Dong Ha, and Dust

I REPORTED TO THE SUPPLY school at Montfort Point in December 1966 in just enough time for us to spend our first Christmas together in a one-story duplex on Onslow Drive in Jacksonville. Our new home had a smelly oil burner that we were convinced was going to blow up every time the noisy contraption rattled on. We had certainly traded down from our place in Woodbridge. I completed the school in about three months, and our stay at Camp Lejeune was brief. One of the most noteworthy events that occurred during our time there was the very first Super Bowl in Los Angeles.

The world was now inexhaustibly consumed with Vietnam. Washington kept dispatching more and more troops. Protests continued to erupt everywhere. Even the new wunderkind, Muhammed Ali, was stripped of his boxing title because he refused to serve. The Arab-Israeli Six Day War flared up in June. In July, some seven thousand national guardsmen were called out to quell riots in Detroit. Ralph Nader published his landmark book *Unsafe at Any Speed*. Could miniskirts go any higher? Of course; and Twiggy was there to show us how.

My orders arrived, and as expected, I was headed to Southeast Asia. The biggest surprise, though, was that I had been assigned to the First Marine Air Wing. Maybe I'd be a pilot after all? We decided that Joyce would be best off spending my thirteen-month tour back home in Pittsburgh with her mother and father. We took some leave and visited both sets of parents in Framingham and Pittsburgh. After some diffi-cult good-byes, we set out for the Staging Battalion at Camp Pendleton in Oceanside, California. It was just the three of us; Joyce, me, and Dubonnet, our schizophrenic midnight-black cat, riding along in our elegant beige 1964 Mercury Comet, which Joyce brought to the mar-riage. She still claims that is why I married her. Well, it was paid for.

We did our best to approach the drive across country as a vacation and avoid saying much about the ultimate reason for the trip. We had a very en-joyable journey. The government was very liberal with travel and leave days, so we were able to take our time and see the sights. I will not forget peering out the window of the remarkable Bright Angel Lodge at the magnificent void that is the Grand Canyon. The only downer I recall was getting "coun-try-boy'd" by a slick service station operator in Tucumcari, New Mexico, who convinced me our lives would be imperiled if I drove one more mile on our shock absorbers. An unexpected hundred and twenty-five bucks or so took a big chunk out of a second lieutenant's salary in those days.

Staging Battalion had been established to comply with a national law that no US serviceman could be sent permanently into a combat zone without a certain minimum number of days of training. We took a room at a little motel next to the beautiful white sand of Oceanside Beach for the month or so that I would be at Camp Pendleton. The training itself was of little practical benefit that I could discern. I actual-ly served as a platoon commander leading my troops mostly on runs up and down the many hills at that large base. Finally, on the 6th of April 1967, I kissed my tearful lady good-bye at the Marine Corps Air Station at El Toro, which is just north of Pendleton, and boarded a Continental Airlines flight bound for Kadena, Okinawa, with a brief stop in Hawaii. Joyce's parents had flown out to meet her so they could accompany her back to Pittsburgh on that long, lonely drive. On April 8, again courtesy of Continental Airlines, I arrived in the city of Da Nang, Republic of South Vietnam.

Wide-eyed and alert, with no idea what to expect, I can remember having an impulse to be ready to duck as I walked down the stairs of the airliner, which did not hang around very long. Rocket and mortar attacks on the airstrip were rare but not unheard of. I reported in to the adjutant and was directed to a bunk in a nearby "hooch" for the night. A hooch was a rectangular, barracks-like wooden building with a gabled sloped sheet metal roof, plywood floor, and screened-in sides. I did note that it had been liberally sandbagged on either side.

As I lay there on my bunk that very first night, it gradually dawned on me that I had finally arrived. We all had been obsessed with the idea of Vietnam for several years. Now I was actually there. Jerry and Charlie were back in Florida, flying planes and relaxing on the beach. It would be fully two years before their chance would come.

The next morning, I was informed that I was to become the supply officer for squadron HMM-363 within Marine Air Group 16. The squadron consisted of CH-34 helicopters, which were those old, tear drop-shaped Sikorsky single rotor birds, which had been retired from every other branch of service except the USMC years before. The squadron was located at the Dong Ha base about 80 to 90 miles north and 10 miles from the Demilitarized Zone and North Vietnam. A chopper was scheduled to pick me up that morning.

No military, I suppose, could operate if all men were given a total and free choice of where they would like to work. Correspondingly, assignments are supposed to be made so as to most efficiently match qualifications with unit needs. I really didn't know what to expect with the helicopter squadron, but it did seem kind of cool at the time. I knew less than nothing about their supply system, but I could learn. So much of anyone's experience in the service depends on this roll of dice of who needs what, when. Al Buescher, a grunt friend from TBS, told me that when he reported in, much as I did, the assignment officer told him that there were four new second lieutenants that he was going to place in units the next day. He said that one of them would be disappointed. The implication was that there were only three rifle platoon slots open. Sure enough, Al drew the short straw and ended up running a sentry dog platoon at Chu Lai. The three other "lucky" Marines went to rifle platoons, and all were killed in combat. You just never know.

As promised, a CH-34 from HMM-363 showed up and I hopped on through the square side door. We left the hot and dusty Da Nang Air Base complex and flew north over lush, green jungles dotted with numerous rice paddies. The day was bright and clear, and the hot air rushed through the plane. A gunnery sergeant crew chief sat across from me and smiled. The clatter of the engine made trying to talk impossible. I was now about to earn my paycheck for the first time. That part was exciting.

On the other hand, as I stared out at that wild but hauntingly beautiful country below me, I thought about all the enemy troops hidden down there who would like to see me harmed, or better yet, killed The impersonal nature of it all suddenly hit me. Why? I'd never met them, and vice versa. I didn't even know them. Was I supposed to feel the same way: kill them on sight as soon as possible? I guess so, but something just didn't compute about the whole arrangement. Maybe I was beginning to understand war for the first time.

I am not sure I was especially effective at my job, but it didn't take me too long to feel like for the first time I actually belonged to a real USMC organization. HMM-363 was mostly staffed by pilots to fly the dozen or so choppers we tried to keep airworthy. The CH-34 was ancient but had a long record of very reliable performance under difficult combat conditions. The pilots liked them because they sat high in the front, with a lot of engine and helicopter directly under their seats, which helped to stop small arms fire from below. The newer, sleeker CH-46 left the pilots completely exposed underneath where they sat.

*One of our birds at HMM 363, a Sikorsky CH 34,
often used for Medevac and recon inserts*

We constantly had aircraft out of service for a variety of reasons, and lost several of them during missions while I was there. Fortunately, most of the accidents were non-fatal, and generally caused by pilot error under difficult conditions, often under fire. We flew field resupply, medevac, recon team inserts, and other types of missions as needed.

*June 1967 finally a real job with CH 34 helicopter squadron in Dong Ha,
Republic of Vietnam, just a long grenade toss from the DMZ and North Vietnam*

On one occasion, one of our birds was sent to resupply the "rock pile," which was a narrow stone hilltop in the far northwest corner of the country, not far from Khe Sanh. A Marine Corps squad occupied the position as an observation post. The area was so small that our pilots could only position the front two wheels on the ground while hovering with the rest of the aircraft. It was a tough maneuver, and sure enough, didn't go so well that day. The helicopter ended up rolling down the rock pile as a total loss. Incredibly, somehow, no one was seriously injured. During that period in 1967, there were plenty of enemy around, but most were Vietcong irregulars, who were bad enough. By the end of the year, however, the much better equipped and trained North Vietnamese Army troops began arriving in large numbers. Things got much hotter when they showed up.

Dong Ha was located on a hot and dusty plain a few miles inland from the South China Sea. Our compound was completely surrounded by wire and functioned as a base for our squadron, as well as a jumping off spot for infantry operations in the DMZ and northwest corner of I Corps, which was the designation given to the upper portion of South Vietnam. The delta region way to the south near Saigon was V Corps, with three regions in between. Our squadron occupied a cluster of hooches where we worked, slept, and ate. My office was in the S-4 shop.

Certain local Vietnamese were allowed to come into the perimeter through the gate to our area on a daily basis. In fact, they operated a laundry in a hooch right next to my office. Prior to my arrival, the base at Dong Ha had never been attacked. In fact, our bunkers were only half-dug. No one bothered to finish them. Bad mistake.

A week or two after I arrived, I noticed that our laundry folks had not shown up that morning. I didn't think much about it. That evening, though, all hell broke loose. I snapped awake to the wailing sound of the attack siren and violent explosions very close by. I grabbed my .45, ran out the door, and leaped into our half-finished hole, along with several other guys. We kept our heads down and huddled together as a barrage of rocket and mortar rounds fell all around us, one or two close enough to shower us with dirt. The noise was deafening. The rounds stopped after a few minutes but we sat tight, hoping that there was not going to be a ground attack into our base as well. We did hear that there was some probing of the wire but no real attempt was made to overrun our position.

Papa San and Son San: skivvies by day rockets by night

You can bet that the first thing we did the next day was to finish off and properly sandbag the bunker. The siren did scream often for several nights after that, and there were additional rocket attacks. I guess it was a total coincidence that we would get hit every time the laundry crew were out sick?

Once the bunker was finished, I actually got to the point that I was more afraid of my fellow Marines squeezed in there with me. They carried all manner of weapons, and sitting there in the dark, always felt compelled to cram live magazines into rifles that were just a few inches from my nose. The fear of friendly fire is an ever present concern in a battle area.

One of the advantages of being with a helicopter group is that you can get around a bit, and I did make several trips back and forth to Marble Mountain Air Facility in Da Nang for various reasons. The Marble Mountain base was a helicopter only field, which had been created on a strip of beach five miles away when the Da Nang Air Base got overcrowded. Hitching a ride on whatever was going was pretty easy.

One day I flew down there in one of our choppers. The reason for the trip was to pick up two more CH-34s that had been repaired and rehabbed and were waiting to be placed back in service. I was standing on the mat area talking to a sergeant from our squadron not far from the maintenance hangar where the choppers had been repaired. We were chatting and watching while one of our pilots tested one of the "repaired" aircraft. The craft raised up and began to hover probably ten feet or so above the ground, maybe fifty to seventy-five yards from where we stood. Then, without any warning, the helicopter pitched violently to starboard and smashed down into the metal mat just below it. All hell broke loose. We drove for the ground as a cloud of acrid black smoke belched out of the struggling machine, which was now beating itself to death as the rotors thrashed against the metal. Pieces flew everywhere. Several struck and wiped out other helicopters nearby that were tied down awaiting service. It ended almost as quickly as it had begun with the dead, helpless bird laying there in a smoldering mess with virtually no rotors left. Again, lady luck was with us that day. The testing pilot miraculously walked away without a scratch. We then got on the other "reconditioned" CH-34 and flew back to Dong Ha. I held my breath the entire trip.

CHAPTER 28

Garrison Living in the City of Brotherly Love

COMPARED TO MY INFANTRY CONTEMPORARIES operating out in the boonies, despite an occasional dash for cover to avoid "incoming," I had it relatively good at Dong Ha. A year or so later, though, after I was long gone, the base was completely overrun by the NVA. Nonetheless, it was still a combat field location where the heat, dust, grime, and dirt had become such a part of your everyday life that you simply accepted such conditions as normal. In a way, it was like being back at Lambda Chi again.

One day I took a chopper ride out to the USS *Princeton*, which was a few miles offshore in the sapphire-blue South China Sea. The *Princeton* was a small carrier designed to handle helicopters. As I walked around the air-conditioned and sparkling-clean spaces on the ship, I could not believe how strange and grungy I felt. Of course, it was right back to reality on shore, but I was able to grab a hot lunch in the ward room and did make a huge score at the ship's store. I nailed a whole box of my then favorite Havatampa cigars with the chewable sweet wooden holders. I wonder if they still make them.

I have mentioned how much luck seems to play in our ultimate fate, especially when it comes to high-risk combat situations. For reasons I have never been able to explain, someone was watching over me, who was working in far, far less perilous circumstances than many of my TBS classmates in country. Even at that, however, danger is all around in combat environments.

One day I was again headed back down to Da Nang for some reason, but none of our choppers were available. In order to make the trip, I ended up catching a ride on a KC-130 four-engine transport that was busy shuffling all the gear of an infantry unit back and forth between Dong Ha and Marble Mountain. There was a short airstrip next to our Dong Ha base where I'd go to catch my ride. I suppose for the obvious reason of ready access to transportation, a "collection and clearing" platoon was operating right next to where I was waiting. A collection and clearing platoon has the almost inconceivable but critical job of identifying the corpses of fallen servicemen and then preparing their remains for shipment back home. There, just a few yards from where I was standing, there were literally piles of dozens of dead Marines, swollen and rotting in the intense Asian sun. The stench and smell were overwhelming. Some of them were hardly recognizable as human. The rows and piles ebbed and flowed based on the amount of combat activity in the immediate area. I will never forget that sight or smell. I wonder if any of the visiting big wigs from Washington, who would tip-toe into country from time to time on "fact finding" missions, which were really just thinly disguised photo ops, ever saw one of these places. If so, I believe that a push for cessation of hostilities would have commenced. Immediately

I caught my hop to the south in a KC-130 that was loaded with gear. I sat in a web seat affixed to the side of the aircraft within the cargo bay. It was very uncomfortable, but the trip was brief, maybe a half-hour or so. Both landing strips on either end of the KC-130's shuttle were very short, which is no problem for that beautiful and impressive workhorse aircraft, which has the ability to hit the ground and immediately reverse props to bring it to a screeching stop. Despite the large size, it also had a jet-assisted takeoff capability to get out on constrained strips.

After taking care of my business, I jumped back on the 130 as it headed up north to pick up more gear. I sat in the same type of seat next to a Marine corporal, who was also hitchhiking. On this leg, the cargo bay was empty as the plane returned for another load. I didn't think much about that and tried to doze during the hot, stuffy, bumpy flight. When the plane banked and headed sharply down, I knew we were approaching Dong Ha. We swooped low and touched down with a loud thump. The powerful props were thrown in reverse and the surging plane began to shudder to a stop.

Unfortunately for those of us in the economy section in the otherwise empty cargo area, the loadmaster and his crew had been a little lax in properly stowing all their blocks, tackle, ropes, and chains they use to secure cargo in flight. When the pilot reversed the props to stop, an ugly balled mass of flying, whirling wood and metal was catapulted from the rear of the cargo bay toward the front. This deadly mass of metal missed our noses by inches. Had we not plastered ourselves to the sides of the plane, I have no doubt that we would have been killed just as easily as from a direct hit from a VC rocket. Luck is where you find it.

After four months or so, I felt like I was growing into the job and was beginning to identify with the squadron. I was surprised, therefore, one afternoon when the commanding officer, a major, called me and told me I had orders. What I had yet to learn, of course, was to never get too comfortable anywhere. I was out of my MOS in the air wing, but so what? I had been reassigned back to Okinawa. After I thought it over for just a bit, I told the major that I wanted to stay. He did check with MAG-16, and no soap. Perhaps fate again was smiling at me. I was headed out of the combat zone. I wasn't really anxious to be there in the first place, but since I was already there, I really wanted to stay. I had hoped to have a chance to make a few actual mission flights on the 34s. Sometimes, they permitted ground officers like me to join the flight crews as gunners with the .50 caliber machine guns they carried. I wanted to get a chance to do that, but there was a MAG-16 group rule against ground officers flying. I had been told, however, that the squadron was due to rotate out with the fleet, where that rule was not in place. If I could hang around until then, I might get my chance. And did I mention that you get a spiffy air medal for every five missions you go on? Instead, I was heading back to Camp Butler on Okinawa, where I would become the Camp Property Officer for the Camp Schwab facility. Ray Daley flew helicopters in Vietnam. I didn't. He died. I am still here.

As I traveled back to Okinawa, which is in the Ryukyuan Island chain and is a part of Japan, I continued to ponder the impersonal nature of war. I had been shot at with lethal weapons, which surely could end my life, and which was the intent of the enemy. What was even more bizarre when you consider it, I was just as anxious to end the lives of folks I had never met. Why? I couldn't help but think, "Hey, Mr. VC, NVA, whoever, why are you are shooting at me? I don't even know you. I am not mad at you. And yet you want me dead. Please, just walk on by and I will do the same." It would be totally different if I have an argument with someone and become very agitated at that specific person for a specific reason. I might want to knock his block off, but at least I know why. In Vietnam, I guess because JFK and LBJ wanted the country to look good, I have to go out and want to kill a bunch of poor rice farmers? Being there and surviving is quite another question, but the whole premise of obliterating total strangers is really senseless. But who am I to question something that has gone on for centuries with no prospect of changing real soon?

For the duration of my Westpac tour I was stationed at Camp Schwab in the northern portion of Okinawa overlooking the same beautiful blue South China Sea. Finally, finally I was now involved in clandestine operations critical to the war effort. Yeah, sure. My most pressing responsibilities were counting and keeping track of bunks and oscillating ceiling fans. I lived in a very comfortable BOQ and became reasonably proficient at handball. I really had little contact with the shooting war.

Regimental Landing Team 26's rear element was stationed at Schwab. The forward element of that group, however, was in country at Khe Shan and ended up in the middle of the nasty siege of that beleaguered outpost when the Tet Offensive kicked off in the fall. Over many beers at the O Club bar I heard lots of hair-raising and grim stories from officers who had been there.

Since I had been sent out of RVN, I did not qualify for the cherished rest and relaxation ("R and R") leave. Instead, I was able to wrangle a way to fly Joyce over for what turned out to be three months. I actually met her in Tokyo on Thanksgiving Day. We lived on base in the BOQ until she flew back a few months before my thirteen-month tour was up. Naturally, we had a terrific time. In fact, when I returned home in the spring of 1968, I was not the least bit upset that my wife was already five months pregnant.

My orders directed me to the Marine Corps Inventory Control Point ("ICP") at Broad and Washington streets in south Philadelphia. The ICP had been set up as the heart of the USMC worldwide automated supply system. The facility itself was located in a 1930s vintage converted old ten-story brick factory building. It housed mainframe computers and had numerous rooms filled with rows and rows of desks manned mostly by civilians with a few Marines sprinkled in here and there. The closest real Marine detachment in the traditional sense was at the Marine barracks on the naval base about two miles straight down Broad Street.

My job was to sit in an office managing about ten people who wrestled with voluminous computer printouts trying to match one transaction against another. I had gotten pretty far away from being a commander of a rifle platoon. By and large, while mainly pretty bored, I was dry, warm, and basically safe. The only real risk to my body, other than daily Philly traffic, was from some of the residents near the ICP. Whenever I went out for a run through those streets, I was called every name you could imagine. "Baby killer" was very popular then.

We lived out of the city in Turnersville, New Jersey, and commuted about an hour everyday over the Delaware River Bridge into Center City where the ICP was located. I had actually arrived home from Westpac in May 1968. After some leave time, we moved to southern New Jersey and reported in to the ICP in the middle of June. Our accommodations were super. We had a first-floor, two-bedroom unit in the Friesmill Apartments, which were brand-new. It had a sliding glass door opening to a small patio. We felt like we had really moved up in the world after Bayvue in Woodbridge and New River in Jacksonville, North Carolina. The Marine Corps had an arrangement with the apartments that effectively treated them like base housing for us. I gave up my standard officer BOQ housing allowance, and we otherwise lived there rent-free. Several other officers and staff NCOs also lived there.

In 1968, domestic and world events continued to reflect the instability and uncertainty of the times. The Soviet Union invaded Czechoslovakia. The Reverend Martin Luther King was gunned down on his hotel balcony in West Memphis, Tennessee. Civil unrest was increasing rapidly across the country, as were war protestors. The black power salute provided the defining moment of the Olympic Games in Mexico City. Senator Robert Kennedy was assassinated in Los Angeles. The NVA launched the Tet Offensive, and an army company committed the tragic massacre at My Lai. LBJ finally ended the bombing of North Vietnam. Aristotle Onassis and Jackie Kennedy tied the knot. The first 9-1-1 emergency call center was set up. The Beatles, Stones, and Supremes dominated the pop music charts. Now, here is real news:

the first Big Mac was sold for $.49. Nonetheless, I was still thrilled to be back on American soil, safe and sound, where in just a few short months I would become a father for the first time.

CHAPTER 29

Ray Daley

FIVE DECADES AGO, WE DID not even dream of having today's routinely accepted luxury of instant communication. There were no social media, iPads, cell phones, faxes, e-mail, Twitter, Instagram, Facebook, text messages, Skype, and so on. It was stamped mail, phone, or in person. I guess it was sort of primitive, but I don't remember us feeling short-changed because we didn't know everything immediately. While I was in Vietnam, I was able to talk to Joyce once by way of a rudimentary short wave radio arrangement. You had to plan days ahead and make sure everyone was waiting. At that, atmospheric conditions often wiped out the radio signal. Calls would be patched through, and you might get five minutes of conversation with several operators listening. "What? What, did you say? Over." An operator somewhere would break in. "He said he loves you. Over." "Oh. Me too. Over." As a consequence, other than by occasional letters or word of mouth, we had relatively little information on what our TBS contemporaries had been doing.

TBS was in the rearview mirror by almost a year and a half when I reported to Philadelphia. Most of the Airedales had finished up their basic flight training and were well into their specialties. Due to the exhaustive nature of the flight preparation syllabus, few had gone to RVN yet, but some were about to leave shortly. Jerry and Charlie had gotten their jets and were still in training at such places as Meridian,

Mississippi, and Beaufort, South Carolina. Craig Zimmer had been born during flight school, and the Pigotts had added a son, David, during the same period. I have no doubt that those two daddies were among the proudest anywhere. Ray Daley and Dave Taylor were in helicopters. Ray flew twin-engine CH-46s and Dave flew one of the Corps' newer, bigger, and faster helicopters, the CH-53. Eventually, he moved on and had the honor of being the pilot of Marine One, which accommodates the president from the White House lawn.

Dave left the Corps after a few years. Billy Peters, who remained active for an entire career, became an Osprey pilot. The Osprey was a fixed-wing aircraft with rotatable rotors, which enabled it to make vertical landings and takeoffs. Paul Kelly had completed Basic school and followed Ron Benoit into Force Recon. After the USMC, a few years later Kelly also ended up close to POTUS, with the Secret Service White House detail. None of our close friends' names had appeared in the *Stars and Stripes* yet. Sadly, that was about to change.

It is staggering to look back at the KIA totals for the Vietnam War and to realize just how fate had thrust our group into the very worst of it. Our timing turned out to be dreadful. History indicates that over 58,000 Americans perished in the Vietnam action. That figure includes non-combat, missing, and died in captivity deaths. I was among the first of our TBS class to arrive in Vietnam, which was mid-1967. Jerry and Charlie arrived in 1969. For the three-year period of 1967-1969, there were 11,363, 16,899, and 11,780 deaths respectively for a total of just over 40,000, or almost 70 percent of the grand total. In no other year did the deaths come close to 10,000. During those three morbid years, we were losing over one thousand service people per month, or more than thirty every single day. I lived through it, watched it, and still cannot believe it actually happened. Who in 1962, when we were fuzzy-faced, beanie-wearing freshman, could have predicted that we would be right in the middle of such carnage?

Joyce and I had barely settled into a routine in Turnersville when the first very terrible news reached us. Ray Daley's chopper had gone down in a hot zone on July 3, 1968. He had not survived. Ray was a Naval Academy grad and very dedicated to his job and service to his country. After TBS and flight school, like almost everyone, Ray was ordered to Vietnam. He arrived in late June and reported in to HMM 164, where he was assigned as a pilot of the Sea Knight CH-46 helicopter. A close friend, Skip Cutis, who was also a chopper pilot and a buddy from TBS, saw him just after he arrived in country. He was in good spirits, and had begun to cultivate a new mustache. Ray was wiry and thin and looked much more like the kid next door than the tough jarhead image we all secretly wanted to portray. I doubt the mustache helped very much. At that point he was also preparing for a forward air controller spot with a grunt company out in the bush. His squadron was based at the Marble Mountain air facility near Da Nang, where I had been on several occasions.

According to reports, just a few days after his arrival on what may have been his first actual mission, he was in the co-pilot's seat with Captain James L. Littler III, a seasoned pilot. Their mission that day was a recon insert just a few miles south of the Marble Mountain base in Quang Nam. There were two Ch-46s assigned to do the insert. Ray's aircraft carried nine members of a recon team and two crew members in addition to the two pilots. Two of the recon team, Sergeant Joseph Jones and Corporal William Johnson, had earned Silver Stars just a few weeks before.

Ray's chopper led the way and was first into the landing zone. It touched down and discharged half the team. Tragically, the landing area was completely surrounded by Vietcong hidden in the jungle. The enemy waited until the Marines were on the ground and then let loose with a tremendous withering barrage of small arms and machinegun fire. The team on the ground was pinned down, and their position was unsustainable. They were almost certain to be overrun.

Ray's Ch-46 had lifted back off and safely cleared the zone, but when Captain Littler saw what was happening on the ground, in an incredible act of bravery, he went right back down to rescue the trapped Marines. His valiant action meant exposing his bird to a crushing volume of enemy small arms fire. As they descended back into the hot zone, at about one hundred feet, automatic weapons fire, including likely a rocket-propelled grenade, struck the cockpit and killed Captain Littler. The aircraft then flipped over and crashed into the landing area, where it burst into flames. In doing so, it most likely killed most of the very Marines on the ground they were trying to save. The Vietcong then proceeded to overrun the position and shot any of the Marines who still happened to be alive. Thirteen fine Marines perished in this horrible incident. Ray was caught upside down in his harness. When his body was recovered, his sidearm .45 was empty. He fought right to the end. Words cannot express my admiration for that great man.

We had not known Ray and Nancy Daley well or for a very long time, but the circumstances under which we met at TBS, with combat service looming, created a strong bond among all of us. I cannot and will not ever attempt to express the manifest grief and heartbreak that an immediate family member undergoes upon such a loss. My feelings of anguish cannot begin to compare to their torment. I can only say for my part that I was shaken to the center of my being. We all lived with the possibility that such a tragedy could and probably would happen, but when it did, you understand that there is simply no way to have prepared for the immense sorrow that envelopes you. My old imbued Yankee cold shoulder tactic of ignoring the unpleasant does not work. Of course, you must suck it up and move on, but the same questions echoed around my brain. Why did that have to happen? Why Ray? Why not me? What was our country doing over there?

Ray's crash raised an issue that I have wondered about for some time and was also to become a factor in another loss that was not far ahead. Piloting is an art that is improved and refined with practice. It makes sense to me that the more time a pilot spends in the air at the stick, the better he will be at flying. Layoffs, it would seem, tend to reduce efficiency. The pressure that an enemy presence and ground fire exerts can only magnify the difficulty to control these sophisticated, highly powered aircraft. In Ray's case, he was on perhaps his very first combat mission. Captain Littler, though, was thoroughly seasoned and, according to reports, was due to rotate home shortly. Therein is the troubling issue. Ray Daley had just arrived, and Jim Littler was going home. How unfortunate is it that a man faithfully performs under incredibly trying and dangerous circumstances for almost an entire tour, and then has his life snuffed out just before he is about to return home to his loved ones? By the same token, Ray fell almost immediately. The circumstances seem to indicate that his newness was probably not a factor in his crash, but long layoffs out of the cockpit should certainly be taken into account when making combat assignments. I am also fully aware that squadron commanders in combat areas are very much aware of their pilots' individual flying status and do everything reasonably possible to manage it. The situation is a grim fact of war.

Norman Billip was another member of our TBS class who ended up in the cockpit. I believe Norm was a Midwesterner who had gone to the University of Wisconsin I remember first meeting him on some of the NROTC summer cruises. He was a big, blond guy, not unlike Charlie Pigott, and if I recall correctly, Norm was also loud like Charlie, but I frankly did not know him well. Captain Billip became an A-4 Skyhawk pilot, which is a smaller, single-seat jet attack aircraft that the Marines used. Apparently, he flew the A-4s for about half his time in country and then switched over to single-engine prop-driven spotter planes, which were used for observation, damage assessment, and intelligence gathering. Norm's switch from powerful jets to passive, tiny prop planes would seem to be quite a dramatic transition. I am not sure why he changed aircraft, but then again, things just seem to happen sometimes in the military. No doubt, they needed a pilot there and he volunteered.

Unfortunately, in early May 1969, Norm did not return from a fairly routine mission, which was at least partly over North Vietnam. The weather that day was horrible, with many thunderstorms. Subsequent searches never found his plane, which it was assumed had been forced down in bad weather. Norm Billip perished on his 265th mission. How much did those guys do for their country? He was also getting ready to come home. Could fatigue or war weariness have been a factor in his judgement to take unnecessary risks? We will never know. Many squadrons, very likely including his, had policies of not letting their men go on dangerous missions just before they were due to rotate home. Norm's final mission was not supposed to be an especially dangerous one.

Of course, we moved on after the news about Ray, which is about all you can do. It was an exciting time for us in October 1968 when on the 10th, Owen Whitehead DeLuca came into our lives. It was as thrilling a moment as I have ever had. Of course, nothing is ever quite perfect, and there turned out to be a bit of angst with his birth in that Joyce experienced some complications during the birth at the Philadelphia Naval Hospital. Although it was unpleasant for a while, mother and baby came through it all just fine, and those days are long forgotten. We were tickled with our new addition, who now, by the way, has two youngsters of his own.

Being a dad is terrific, but I honestly had never thought much about grandfatherhood, until it happened to me a few years back. I must say it is a really unique, puzzling, and yet highly gratifying experience. You look down at that bundle of joy and think, "Somehow, some way, I had something to do with that little one being here." Charlie and Jerry at least did have the chance to experience fatherhood firsthand. Once again, why have I been so blessed while they were robbed of having a hand in their kids growing up, maturing, and starting families of their own? My guess is, though, that they have watched it all with great interest from their F4Bs on high.

CHAPTER 30

Escort Duty: What Can You Say?

LIFE AS A GARRISON MARINE was hardly taxing for me. In fact, my daily routine was much more like that of a nine-to-five civilian. The ICP in south Philly was a tall, remodeled former factory that was occupied by several hundred pencil pushers, the vast majority of whom were civil service workers paid under the standard GS schedule. There could not have been more than a company of Marines in the entire place. We did wear our uniforms to work, which set us apart from similar installations in urban locations such as Washington, DC. It also made us ready targets for catcalls and occasional verbal abuse from certain local south Philadelphians. I commuted in from New Jersey in a carpool with other Marines who lived nearby. In general, I was at my desk by 0730 and on my way home fighting traffic by 1930. Nights and weekend duty were the exception rather than the rule.

One morning I was sitting at my desk with a wooden ruler, guiding it down a long list of light-green computer printout entries in a thick binder, when Vince Viscardi, my master sergeant, tapped me on the shoulder and told me that Major Winglass would like to see me. Vince was a wonderful guy and a dedicated career staff NCO. When I think of Vince, I am reminded of an exceptional quality he possessed that I noticed in several other topnotch staff NCOs I had encountered. It is important to understand that the Corps runs on the backs of these vital individuals who have committed their lives to serving. Most have spent as much as 15 to 20 years in and out of combat zones and understand the dynamics of the Maine Corps like no one else. The way the service is structured, however, it is inevitable that, on a regular basis, a dripping wet, green-as-the-grass lieutenant will be inserted in place as their "boss" on the organizational chart. The youngest, latest new lieutenant is superior *on paper* to the most senior 30-year sergeant major. It is a fact of life.

Most of the senior NCOs understand and gracefully accept this peculiar situation that puts young, new officers, who don't know a damn thing, technically in charge over them. So long as the new young guys who happen to have bars on their shoulders are willing to learn, most staff NCOs will take them under their wing and assist them in getting up to speed. Vince was just such a guy. I, who knew absolutely nothing about the Marine Corps stores system, found myself as his boss. Vince knew the drill and was incredibly helpful in bringing me along in a tactful manner that didn't make me look like an idiot.

I would blurt out something like, "Vince, these figures don't even add up!"

He would slowly turn his head while his glasses slipped down on his nose, and peer over at me from his desk with a patient and understanding smile. "You may be right, Captain, but I think if you will flip over to the next page there are some more numbers to include."

"Oh, yes, yes, of course. Thank you, Top," I mumbled back. Vince Viscardi was outstanding.

As I walked back among the gray metal desks to the major's office to see what he wanted, I also thought how fortunate I was to have him as my immediate boss. A New Englander, like me, we had hit it off from the start. He had a quick wit and was always fair, helpful, and understanding. I admired him as a dedicated career Marine. After winking at Rosalie, his secretary, I walked into his office. He was sitting behind his desk reading the *Philadelphia Inquirer* newspaper.

"Those pathetic Red Sox. They blew an eight-run lead to the Yankees, of all people, last night. They stink."

If there were two things that all diehard Red Sox fans agreed on back in those days, they were that, yes, the team sucked, and, further, that we all hated the Yankees, who never seemed to lose. "No argument there, Major. Have you thought about the Phillies?"

"Huh? Come on, Robit, now don't be ridiculous. If we sit here and keep crying about the Sox, we'd better take an early lunch to the closest bar where we can at least drown our sorrows." He reached down on his desk and handed me a manila envelope. "Here you are. This just came over from the adjutant's office."

I reached for the envelope and noticed there was the name of a first lieutenant typed across the top with the letters "NV" scratched in blue ink just below the name. I immediately knew what it was all about. The ICP, which was located in south Philadelphia, was less than 100 miles from the US Mortuary in Dover, Delaware. Dover was the East Coast collection point for all the remains of service personnel shipped home from Vietnam. The Marine Corps had a tradition that any fallen comrade would be accompanied to his final resting place by a fellow Marine. I had just been given orders to go to Dover, meet the remains of that lieutenant, and accompany him home.

"Good luck," the major offered with a woeful half-smile. "That is not fun duty."

It would serve little benefit, even all these years later, for me to identify the fallen Marine or the location where I was to accompany him. I did not personally know him. I will call him "Johnson" from Pennsylvania. I arrived at the mortuary in Delaware a few days later, based upon a schedule such that would put me there when aircraft carrying the remains arrived. A funeral director from his hometown was also there with his hearse. I watched as the casket was unloaded from the aircraft and made certain that the handlers always moved it feet first, as was our custom. The casket was loaded into the hearse, and I rode shotgun as we drove to a small town in central Pennsylvania. This duty, which I was to repeat a few more times, was grim, but I felt a real sense of purpose. I hadn't known the fallen comrade; not that time, at least.

"Body escort" assignments are really fairly simple, if not hopelessly tragic. The Marine Corps instructs you only to accompany the fallen comrade home, after which you are to serve at the convenience of the family. If they want you to stay for the funeral, then you do so. Sometimes they cannot stand the sight of a uniform and want you to leave immediately. In this case, they asked me to stay.

Another wretched complication that arises in such cases is that the remains were marked as "NV," which means "Non Viewable." Most often, so long as the head area can be prepared acceptably, the bodies will not be marked as "NV." It is not hard to imagine the complications an "NV" situation creates. Understandably, the aggrieved wife or parent wants one last look at her loved one. If the medical staff was not able to prepare a viewable head, it is reasonable to assume that the remains are in such a deplorable condition that they do not in any way resemble the man in life. Certainly, no one wants the wife or parent to see that horrible last sight, which she will live with forever. It is far better that their last image of him remain when they last saw him vigorous, alive, and well. The Corps' official policy in such situations is that ultimately, it cannot prevent anyone from unwrapping the remains. On the other hand, we did everything we could to discourage that action, even to the extent of implying that it was not permitted. Still, however, people have read or heard about battlefield mistakes. Perhaps it is not really their loved one in there. They need to be sure.

In this case, despite all our attempts to discourage her, Mrs. Johnson needed to be certain. We were at least able to convince her that she should let her brother actually see him. The funeral director and brother sat down in a room alone with the remains. As he started to unwrap, the brother put a hand on his shoulder and tearfully asked him to stop. He would go out and reassure his sister that it was surely her husband. How many thousands of miles was I from being that innocent college freshman just a few years ago who thought he could play football?

CHAPTER 31

Charlie

FOR MOST AMERICANS, 1969 WILL be remembered for some remarkable achievements, especially the first moon landing. A stoic Neil Armstrong eased down the ladder of the Lunar Module with his blood pressure registering hardly above normal and uttered his famous words. In less than a decade the United States, which started way behind the Russians in the space race, overtook and now far exceeded them. Incredibly, over a half-century later, we remain the only country to ever put a man on another celestial body. Richard Nixon became president, and a throng of 250,000 marched on Washington to demand that we withdraw from Vietnam. The Beatles released their Abbey Road album, which is the last one that they ever completed together. The tiny hamlet of Woodstock, New York, was overwhelmed by an estimated 500,000 avid music lovers, twice the crowd of the Washington march, most dressed with unkempt hair, headbands, and bizarre attire reflecting youth's flourishing anti-establishment feelings. Finally, our troop strength in Vietnam began to be drawn down. Unfortunately, that action came too late for many.

We were approaching our first anniversary in New Jersey when the last group of our TBS class were heading off to Southeast Asia. This contingent was primarily the jet pilots, whose training was longer and more extensive than with other types of aircraft or MOSs. Charlie and

Jerry, who had been trained to fly F4B Phantoms, were included. After Pensacola, they went on to additional training at Meridian, Mississippi, and Beaufort, South Carolina. By the time all their preparation was complete, leave was taken, and travel time was factored in, many of them would not start arriving in Vietnam until early to mid-1969, which was two years after I had stepped off Continental Airlines in Da Nang. In fact, Jerry arrived in country in February 1969 and was assigned to VMFA-542, which was an F4 squadron stationed at the Da Nang Air Base. Just a few months later in mid-May, Charlie arrived and joined the same squadron. I have been told that Jerry did his best and was successful in getting his close friend to be assigned to his unit.

Living in Turnersville, which is in the southern part of the state and very close to the New Jersey Turnpike, we were in a good location to provide overnight way station lodging for travelers heading from the south up to New York or New England. In fact, we were delighted in March when Carol Pigott dropped in with David in tow. Charlie had his orders to Westpac and was in the middle of his leave and travel period. Carol was driving back to New England to see her parents before settling somewhere for the thirteen months that Charlie would be away. Unfortunately, Charlie was driving independently with daughter, Stacey, and we did not get to see them. Carol has always been laid-back, and we enjoyed her visit. We laughed, drank wine, and caught up on the past two years. She and David continued their trip the next morning.

A few months later on an afternoon in the middle of May, I returned to my desk at the ICP and saw a pink phone message slip from "your wife." I sat down, picked up the phone, and called her. "So what's for dinner?" I began as soon as I heard her come on the line. "I hope it is not pasta. I just had spaghetti for lunch."

There was no response to my lame attempt at humor. All I heard were some sniffles and then the unmistakable sound of sobbing.

"What's wrong? Are you okay? Owen?" I blurted back.

"No. No. We are okay. It's Charlie. He crashed in Vietnam."

"Is, is he okay?" I pleaded, already knowing the answer.

"He was killed. His plane crashed into another one. Several Marines were lost. One of the other wives here heard about it. It is terrible. I feel so bad for Carol and the kids. What will they do?"

I told her not to worry. I would try to find out more details, and we would talk about them when I got home. There wasn't much more to say right then. As I hung up the receiver, I stared at it as an overwhelming feeling of shock and helplessness washed over me. I didn't want to believe it. Maybe it was just a rumor that had gotten out of hand. I knew Charlie had just arrived in country. I didn't think he'd even been there long enough to be back in the air.

As an officer and a professional in the Marine Corps during this period of time, you had to expect that there would be casualties. It absolutely came with the job, but it still didn't make it any easier when a close friend was involved. You had to suck it up and move on. Much easier said than done.

I hadn't seen or even talked to Charlie Pigott for over two years, but that was of no consequence whatsoever. We'd both been busy serving our country and the USMC in widely different directions. The next time I would have seen him, it would have been no different than if I'd sat with him for lunch at Brown after having last seen him in class a few days earlier. Charlie had no pretense about him. I would have expected, perhaps, that he might at least have referred to me as "Captain Eight ball," but I would have been glad to see him under any circumstances. I felt totally empty and disheartened. Why did that guy who was so full of life have to be taken so early? I just didn't understand then, nor I have I figured it out yet. As I mentioned before with Ray Daley, our own profound sense of loss and grief still cannot approach that of Charlie's loved ones and family.

In researching Charlie's crash, I became aware that there may be certain aspects of the tragedy that were controversial. I have no interest in contributing to any such questions in any way. I will attempt only to describe the basic horrible incident as I understand it. Fate often plays such a sturdy hand in such accidents that I am convinced that laying blame is essentially a fool's errand. The odds of two powerful aircraft piloted by accomplished professionals colliding in the huge expanse of open airspace is minute. There is, frankly, a much better, but still infinitesimal chance, of a senior citizen's church bus slamming into a concrete bridge abutment at 70 miles per hour. The bus routinely passes by obstructions by only a few feet. Any swerve or slight change in steering direction would create a disaster every bit as horrible as the aircraft incident. Neither should ever happen, but sometimes they do.

Charlie was in the cockpit on May 18, 1969, as pilot of F4B Phantom (Bu No. 151001) with Captain John Nalls from Washington, DC, as his radar intercept officer. The flight that day was to familiarize Charlie with the squadron's aircraft, the area, and give him a few hours back at the stick after the long break from training command to his arrival in country. It was his second hop after reporting to the squadron. Knowing Charlie, I am sure he was anxious to start flying regular missions. It was early afternoon. The day was clear as he taxied out on the Da Nang Air Base tarmac, received his clearance, and took off on what ended up being a northward bearing.

During the morning of that same day, Major Jimmy Sells had been operating his KC-130 (Bu No. 148892) four propeller-driven tanker up and down the coast of I Corps out over the water. The KC-130 was part of VGMR 152 out of Ubon, Thailand, and besides the pilot, Major Sells, the aircraft carried a co-pilot and crew of four. The tanker's mission was to fly a Barrier Combat Air Patrol, "BARCAP", route up and down the coast while refueling jet fighters as needed on an air-to-air basis. Major Sells had actually put down for lunch at DaNang and taken off again at just after noon. He was due to come off station a 1330. His plane was refueling two F4Bs with drogue hoses while flying south just off Hue-Phu Bai. He was using a method known as tobogganing, during which the larger and slower tanker actually dives to pick up speed so that the faster refueling fighter jets don't overrun it.

For reasons that can only be explained by the fickleness of fate, Charlie's plane, which was still in climb out from the Da Nang Air Base heading north, flew directly into the KC-130 at about 700 knots airspeed. The Phantom struck the fourth engine of the tanker, causing debris to impact the cockpit of the tanker, which immediately became uncontrollable and crashed into the South China Sea below, killing the crew of six. Charlie's plane also crashed into the water. Neither man was able to eject. Both of the Phantoms that were refueling were able to break away. One of them was too damaged to remain airworthy, and both the pilot and rear observer did eject and were rescued. The other Phantom successfully made it back to Chu Lai where it landed safely. In all, eight valiant Marines perished during that horrible afternoon. I suppose the only certain conclusion is that it is unlikely that enemy action played any role.

I was a little surprised when Major Winglass called me in and handed me another manila envelope. It had "Captain Charles W. Pigott" printed across the top and "NV" was annotated in blue ink. Based on the circumstances of his crash, I was a little surprised, since I assumed that there would probably not be any remains to recover. Carol had specifically requested that I be assigned the body escort duty, and I was deeply honored to comply. Charlie would be buried with full military honors in Arlington National Cemetery. The funeral would be held on June 6, 1969, exactly three years from our graduation and commissioning date. While I was very familiar now with the body escort routine, my duties in this case would actually be much less than normal. The tragic fact was that there had been so many military funerals in the national cemetery it had become a virtual production line. I am in no way demeaning that hallowed ground where so many of our nation's best found their last resting places. On the other hand, some of the private small-town services I have attended seemed so much more personable.

With dress blues packed, Joyce and I drove to Dover where we met the remains and escorted them to a temporary holding place in Arlington. Perhaps I am a bit harsh in this regard, but my dealing with death during this period of my life convinced me that the physical remains contained in a casket are just that: remains. I truly believe that the person's spirit has already moved on, hopefully to a much better place. Charlie was not in that box. He was already in heaven, probably getting drinks for people with his fingers in their glasses.

Nonetheless, an Arlington funeral with full military honors is an occasion to behold and, in fact, stretches very deeply into the richest traditions of this great country. That day in June was warm and humid, as I recall. We were happy to receive a slight puff of wind every so often. The cemetery grounds were beautiful, with green, manicured rolling hills, abundant old hardwoods, and thousands of rows of white crosses and stone monuments. Charlie's casket was draped with an American flag and positioned on a horse-drawn caisson, which is trailed by an escort platoon of Marines that marches to the final resting place. In Charlie's case, he ended up in Section 46, which is near the center of the cemetery, very close to the Battle of the Bulge Monument in World War II, during which I lost an uncle. His remains are also resting not far from the western boundary with Fort Meyer and Henderson Hall, which happens to be the headquarters for the entire USMC. I had gone there the previous day to read the official account of the accident.

Once the casket reached the gravesite, it was carried from the caisson and gently and respectfully set down by a detail of Marine pallbearers. After all these years, one of my still outstanding memories of that morning was that one of those Marines had failed to shave that day and looked very sloppy. I took that very personally, and felt he was being disrespectful to my friend. For once I held my tongue. Perhaps it was the emotion of the whole thing.

The firing party executed the salute, and the lonely bugler's taps echoed throughout the field. There are few moments in a military man's life that are more haunting. The flag draped over Charlie's casket was removed and smartly folded thirteen times into the symbolic triangular shape. It was presented to Carol with the following words:

"On behalf of the president of the United States, the Commandant of the Marine Corps, and a grateful nation, please accept this flag as a symbol of your loved one's service to this Country and the Corps."

Charlie was gone. I don't remember much of what I said to Carol at that time. There was not much that could be said.

McDonnell-Douglas F4B Phantom
(May differ from those used by VMFA 542 in RVN)

CHAPTER 32

Jerry

⤴

IT SEEMS ODD TO SAY that you feel lonely when you are sitting in a car next to the most important person in your whole world, but that was what I felt as Joyce and I drove back up to Philadelphia from Arlington. I hadn't seen Charlie for a couple of years, and yet I felt as though a piece of me was missing. Fortunately, there was still so much to do that life doesn't let you stay in a hangdog posture very long. Carol, by the way, bundled up the kids and moved from New England to sunny southern California, where she eventually remarried. Elaine was living in Smithfield, Rhode Island.

Jerry continued to fly missions in and around the northern corps of South Vietnam, mainly in support of ground troops, who dearly appreciated what the "fast movers," as the jets were referred to as, could do to make their combat lives more tolerable. He had been made a section leader and was certainly one of the more competent pilots in the group. I never got a chance to talk to Jerry about Charlie, but I am certain that, although he was devastated, he soldiered on and did his job to the best of his ability.

For at least part of his tour, he was able to fly twenty-four missions with his buddy from home, Gene Mares, who also was a member of VMFA-542. Jerry and Gene, who actually went back to when they were eight years old, were good friends in high school, and Jerry was responsible for recruiting Gene to become a radar intercept officer (RIO) in the F4 program. Gene was best man in their wedding.

In New Jersey, we were about back to normal when the dog days of summer took over. It was late August, and I think I had been firing on the range, which was in southern New Jersey not far from Turnersville, for my annual qualification. In those days, of course, there were no cell phones, and pay phones were few and far between. I arrived home late in the afternoon still dressed in my Marine green utilities from having spent a hot, dusty day shooting. I was sweaty, tired, and thirsty. I pulled our Chevy Malibu into the parking space right in front of our apartment, which was on the first floor.

As I started to get out, our apartment door opened. Joyce looked at me and just stood there with moist and doleful eyes. I knew. I just knew. It was only three months or so since the news about Charlie, and just a little over two since his funeral. I prayed I was wrong. I prayed she had burned our dinner or wasted twenty bucks of money we didn't have on something we didn't need. I didn't dare think about little Owen. All that was not to be. The third member of our little VW excursion to Virginia a few years back had now gone to join Charlie.

I grabbed her and squeezed tight. Again, it just didn't seem possible. Not Jerry; he always came out on top in the end. He was so strong-willed he just would not fail in whatever he attempted. I immediately thought of his reassuring me when I had creeping doubts about the Marine Corps. Jerry was no Charlie, who would bang things into submission if necessary to prevail. But not Zim. He had a little Davey Crockett in him. "Be sure you're right and then go ahead." Don't bother looking back, because you are absolutely going to succeed. For the second time in less than ninety days, we were too shocked to function. We just stood there holding on. I guess it was lucky that little ten-month-old Owen was inside and very hungry. His bellowing finally brought us around enough to at least go inside.

Losing Charlie had been tough, but at least we had Jerry still over there doing what they both had trained to do. It wasn't like we would have been there when he stepped off the plane when he came back, but at least a part of what we'd all been through was still there. We were sure someday, somewhere, we'd get together, reminisce, and hoist a few to old Chaz, who I am sure wouldn't mind. But now even that was out. Both of those two courageous Americans, wonderful husbands, caring fathers, and tremendous friends, would never be returning. Why them? They simply deserved a much better fate.

Now the fruitless war was actually winding down, and we lost two of our most precious people. I have since wondered how the loved ones of Marines Charles McMahon and Darwin Judge felt when they were killed at the fall of Saigon in April 1975 and were the very last combat casualties of the entire bloody episode. Why were we still there at all? Pretty clearly, we couldn't win on the ground. It was obviously for political and saving face reasons. Ord Elliot, a grunt, who was also in our class at TBS has written a book called *The Silent Warrior*. He managed to live through some pretty amazing operations and personally witness the loss of many close friends and men under and over him. He has suggested that we should have let Robert McNamara, the erudite Secretary of Defense, walk the point on patrol for about a half-hour. Everyone would have been home soon.

Jerry had been in country with VMFA-542 just about six months when on August 29, he and his radar intercept officer, First Lieutenant Al Graf, a Georgian, were sitting on the tarmac in F4B Phantom (Bu. No. 150341) in an on call ready status to quickly respond to any requests for close air support from Marines operating on the ground. Sure enough, a call came through at noon from Quang Nam Province, which by coincidence was where Ray Daley was killed. As they had done many times before, they ran a quick checklist, snapped their visors, taxied out, and took off to assist Marines on the ground.

The hot spot was only about twenty miles to the south, and they were on station very quickly. Second Lieutenant Wayne Rollings, who would eventually go on to become a Brigadier General and be awarded the Navy Cross for valor, was leading a recon team in the Que Son Mountains. He had asked for the close air support to clear a landing zone for a recon team insert. Jerry and Al swooped in and dropped their first 500-pound bomb. After releasing the ordnance, for reasons that have never been entirely clear, their aircraft did not pull up, and crashed into the side of a mountain covered with dense jungle. The plane had most likely been hit by automatic weapons fire, probably .50 caliber, which rendered Jerry unable to keep control. Neither Jerry nor Al Graf were able to eject. Recovery attempts at the time, which were limited by the terrain and enemy activity, failed to locate the actual crash site. Neither of the bodies was recovered, and both were listed as MIA. Elaine and Jerry had been scheduled to meet for R&R very shortly.

As with all my unfortunate friends, I appreciate from the depths of my being the heartache that loved ones suffer in that situation, but I will make no attempt to discuss it here. In Jerry's case, the matter was further complicated by the sad fact that they were not able to recover his body. Elaine could not even have a traditional funeral, but did choose to have a memorial service on the farm in New York where Jerry had been raised. Without the actual physical final confirmation of the tragedy, a myriad of other complications and issues arise, to say nothing of prolonging the grief period by extending closure indefinitely. In most cases, the horror of these tragedies does abate over time, once the fallen hero is put to rest. In Jerry's case, the wound remained open. Speculation is inevitable. Did he perish in the crash? Was he alive after the crash? Could quick rescue action have saved him? Maybe he survived the crash and was captured. Is he a prisoner somewhere? Is he wandering out in the jungle? Under the circumstances, none of these possibilities seems likely, but they could not be ruled out totally. As dreadful as a funeral can be, at least all those open questions are laid to rest with the interment.

Elaine Zimmer reacted, I suppose, much like Carol Pigott had under similar circumstances. She packed up and moved off to California with two-year-old Craig. It is logical that she would feel comfortable to locate around other military people who could relate to her circumstances. In fact, she eventually met and married another Marine pilot, of all people, who had flown helicopters in combat in Vietnam. Ron Davis could certainly understand her situation. They have now been married some forty years and have a son of their own. Elaine has addressed her grief for Jerry in a fascinating way. She has made it her lifelong quest, even after all these years, to locate Jerry's body in the jungles south of Da Nang and bring him home. She is joined in this passionate effort by Ron. Together they have become an effective team in spearheading this gallant effort. Everyone knows that Marines do not leave their fallen on the battlefield, and Jerry Zimmer should be no exception.

The struggle to recover Jerry Zimmer and Al Graf has taken on a life of its own and has seen Elaine wage battles on many fronts. She has urged, cajoled, and pressed the ponderous United States bureaucracy to increase and sustain their limited efforts to find and return the some 2,500 veterans who are listed as missing in Vietnam. Many have been found and were finally accorded their long-past-due military honors. She has traveled to Vietnam and hiked over hills and the steaming, humid jungles to get close to the very site where they believe Jerry went down. They even found pieces that must have been a part of his Phantom. Her efforts seemed just about to finally pay off, when the funding for MIA recovery excavation dried up. She has had to appeal to whoever would listen to her about her case. Even though a large part of the probable crash site has been excavated, to date, no remains have been found. Elaine continues to be steadfast in her conviction that she will not rest until every inch of the site has been thoroughly searched. Her determination and hope have never wavered. There is no question that she will prevail. Short of the actual recovery, Elaine's efforts to date to *"Bring Jerry Home"* are not without impressive accomplishments. She has been an outspoken standard bearer for all those who have lost loved ones under similar circumstances.

After giving due thought to remaining on active duty after my initial four years, which satisfied my obligation to Uncle Sam, we decided to leave the service in June of 1970. I took a position as a management trainee with the Mellon Bank in Pittsburgh, Pennsylvania which was where Joyce had grown up. A few years later we moved to the Houston, Texas area, where I worked in various aspects of the real estate industry until I hung things up for good in 2010 or so. Along the way we raised a brood of four terrific sons, who have presented us with ten fantastic grandchildren. I have always treasured my association with the USMC brotherhood, although the time demands of my family and pursuit of my livelihood kept me away from much direct contact with anyone from back in those days for many years.

In August 2009, we received some encouraging news, Elaine was able to arrange for Jerry to have a full memorial service at Arlington in a special section reserved for service members missing in action. When his remains are found, he will be interred in a burial section of the cemetery. Joyce and I flew in from Houston and attended the beautiful service on yet another hot and blustery day, along with Jerry's immediate family members and friends, some of whom were from Brown. Full honors were accorded with a horse-drawn caisson, rifle salute, and taps. Craig Zimmer, Jerry's son, received the flag. Jerry's monument is positioned right next the one for Al Graf. As a father of four sons, I cannot begin to describe the cherished sensation that overwhelmed me watching Craig that day. Although he is now more than twice the age of Jerry when I last shook his hand on the parade deck at TBS graduation, his son's image, mannerisms, and overall demeanor are undeniably those of his fallen dad.

After leaving Arlington, Joyce and I drove up the East Coast to Massachusetts to visit my then ninety-one-year-old mother and other members of my family in the New England area. Among the special people we saw on that trip was my aunt Amelia Dugas. "Auntie Mi," as we always have known her, is the eldest of five children, which included my father in the middle and four sisters. She was living with her two sisters, Evelyn and Diane, in a pleasant single-family detached home in Garden City, Rhode Island, where she had lived for perhaps the past forty years. Amelia was ninety-three when we dropped in, and eventually made it into her next century. My mother, whom my aunts have always considered a sister, was with us. We were greeted when we arrived by Aunts Amelia, Diane, and Evelyn; just in time, of course, for a typical Italian lunch. The pasta, antipasto, cold cuts, bread, and assorted pastries were loaded all over the dining room table, which was covered with a white linen tablecloth.

"Robit, Robit," I was urged by each of them as they took turns, "Have some more. Try the veal culets. They are very good. Your favorite! We cooked them this morning just for you." I needed little encouragement and, as usual, around them I was too stuffed to even move. Joyce gave me one of those disgusted looks.

"Oh, Joyce, you look so wonderful. You look dahling in that outfit. Robit, you are so lucky." They continued a steady stream of platitudes and open affection on us. "So tell us about the kids."

We spent the next hour or so passing pictures of our kids and grandkids. The trio of aunts loved photos and continued a constant barrage of questions about who, what, where. In just a few years, we would notice that while the affinity for pictures remained high, the same questions would become repeated over and over as mental acuity began to ease. There was finally a pause in the conversation, and Auntie Mi looked over at my mother, who knew exactly what was coming. "Bar-bra, your hair looks good like that . . . but why don't I just give you a little trim?" Auntie Mi suggested. She owned her own hair dressing shop in Providence for decades and still couldn't resist the urge get involved where she could.

I knew my mother did not want her to touch her hair, but also real-ized it would be difficult to refuse. "No, Melia. It's fine like it is," she pleaded, but after seeing my aunt's displeased look replied, "Oh, okay, but don't take much off." I smiled at the exchange and wondered if Joyce was next.

Aunt Diane then asked us why we were on the trip all the way from Texas. I hesitated a bit before answering. I knew what my response would bring from Auntie Mi, but I really didn't have a choice. I explained to them about the memorial service for Jerry Zimmer at Arlington, and how he was a friend of mine at Brown. I glanced over at Evelyn, who had my eye, and we both looked over at Auntie Mi, who had suddenly become quiet for the first time since we arrived. Her eyes were downcast and damp. She looked up and softly said, "Just like my Johnny. Your friend and his wife sound just like us. I am so sorry for her," and looked away.

The year was 2009. Sixty-seven long years before, a young, ener-getic, attractive Amelia DeLuca fell in love with a thin but ruggedly handsome automobile parts salesman. She married her sweetheart, and for all of about six months they had a wonderful life together. They double and triple dated with my parents and Evelyn and her husband, Jerry. My dad was in the Coast Guard and Jerry was in the Army. Sure enough, Johnny Dugas was not about to sit home while others fought for the country in World War II. He also enlisted in the Army, and right after boot camp, he was off to Europe, where he served in the 334th Regiment of the 84th Infantry Division. It was January 1945, and it is not clear if he was in Belgium or Germany with his unit fighting at the

Battle of the Bulge. In any event, records indicate that he was killed in combat on January 24, 1945. He had just arrived in December 1944, and all hostilities ended around the first of May 1945. Once again, he showed up just to be in the wrong place at the wrong time. But for a couple of months . . .

Amelia was distraught and devastated when the horrible telegram reached her. There would be no body returned to this United States; he was interred in France. And then, a very peculiar thing happened. She received a letter from him that was dated *after* the date of death in the telegram. Her heart leapt! Could there have been a mistake? Was he really still alive somewhere in Europe? The fog of war. Communications were all but non-existent during that time. She dared hope that some news would come through and resolutely and faithfully attended Mass every single day for the next year. But, of course, no more news ever came, and she had to accept the terrible truth that he was not coming back.

While she has always carried the memory of "her Johnny" close to her heart, she decided to devote her life to helping others and has been incredible in doing so. I am not sure if she ever even had another date, but certainly never married again. She became a second mother to my sister, brother, five cousins, and me. She could not do enough for us. She took my cousin and me on the overnight sleeper train to New York to stand in the window and be seen on TV on Dave Garraway's *Today* show. We ate at the automat, which we'd heard about, but couldn't believe really existed. At every Christmas she bought presents not only for us but also for us to give to our parents. As a hairdresser, she always had lots of tip cash. I never was near her when I didn't get some loose change or dollar bills pressed into my hand. While I was at Brown, she did all my laundry and always supplied me with pizza and pasta for half the fraternity. Movies, toys, Encyclopedia Britannica, you name it. She was always pleasant and thrilled to see us. When she visited our home, she immediately grabbed a broom, mop, or her scissors and had at it. She cared nothing for herself. She was incredible.

So, I suppose, everyone deals with tragic losses in their own way. As I write this story I can now tell you that my auntie Mi has finally been reunited with her Johnny after losing him over seventy years ago. In February 2016, she cracked the century mark, but just a few months later in April the Lord called her home. Up to the very end she still lit up the room whenever she entered at the nursing home. We all wanted her to stay with us long as was possible, and we miss her tremendously. She is gone but will never be forgotten. Her passing is bittersweet; but at the same I am ecstatic that she is finally back with her Johnny. Auntie Mi was never one to sit around. I'll bet she is making the rounds up there. In fact, I'll bet she even goes by and says hi to Jerry and Charlie, first chance she gets. I hope they have kept their hair cut.

We made a trip recently to the pristine wilderness that is the Denali National Park in central Alaska and were fortunate to take a bus tour with a sagacious fellow about our own age. Like many of the folks we encountered up there, this man works only for the precious few summer months when the weather is tolerable. For most of the year he returns to southern California, where I have no doubt that at one time he embraced the hippie lifestyle with the best of them. His shoulder-length, thinning blond hair is certainly a vestige from those days. Blessed with the gift of gab, he proved very entertaining and shared a number of deep insights about the preserve in particular, as well as life in general during the couple of hours or so we spent rumbling around with him. Moose, elk, bears, mountains, and the like. Guide Gary said one thing that made perfect sense to me. On the sixties, he reflectively opined, "If you can remember them, you probably weren't there." You know, that just about says it all.

CHAPTER 33

Forty Years for a Thank You

IT SEEMS LIKE ONLY YESTERDAY that we were hoisting dimey drafts at the Crystal Tap at the bottom of the hill in Providence or trying to block out Roger Lamphear's epithets and tongue lashings during a forced march on the infamous hill trail at TBS in Quantico. The crushing reality is that, in fact, half a hundred years have slipped through the hourglass since those days. Way back then in the 1960s, I am guessing that few of us would have expected to make it this far, but somehow, Vietnam, and all, most of us did. After all, we were a special group. Just to earn those precious gold bars in 1966, every lieutenant had to be exceptional in many ways. Most of us were also fast, loose, and impatiently eager to see and do. We didn't waste a lot of time worrying about next week, next month, or even next year. There was a country to protect, war to win, family to raise, civilian job to get, partying to do, and a whole wide world to explore. There was no retreat, literally and figuratively, for young Marines. Always onward and upward.

Oh, my, how that has changed. With families raised and fortunes (?) secure, those of us who matriculated through B Company in the class designated TBS 1-67 are certainly not today idle, sedentary, or moribund. The forty or so ex-jarheads who posed for a photo on a set of bleachers at the 50th reunion at The Basic School recently are for the most part hale, hearty, and full of life. Still, though, there is no denying that the edge is off the blade. The finish is much closer than the start. There is no reason to be glum. In fact, we are now in a unique position to reflect back on almost an entire lifetime. It is true that much of the competitive, assertive, and even combative aspects of our lives as young officers are fleeting, but in our later years there has been a transformation that may have caught us unaware. Our pride in having served has always been manifest, but now that sacred period a half-century ago has become even more special. We still take enormous pride in all the obvious trappings of the Corps such as the eagle, globe, and anchor, pomp and circumstance, flashy uniforms, parades, and/or even the inherent satisfaction of having been a part of the best fighting organization in the history of the world. Yet something else has become increasingly clear. We can now finally understand and appreciate the superb quality of collective content of the character embodied by those incredible men with whom we stood in formation during one the most turbulent times in our country's history.

Perhaps twenty years ago now, Bob Schmidt, a TBS-167, B company classmate, decided to see how many of the one hundred eighty-one of us he could locate. When I received the first inquiry I was quite happy to respond and add my contact information to his list. There was discussion about getting together, reunions, etc., which I discounted as something "old men" do. I was still much too preoccupied otherwise. As the years passed, however, Bob's kernel of an idea germinated when classmates such as Andres Vaart, Bob Lange, Larry Karch, Hon Lee, and several others pitched in. Now only a very few of us remain undiscovered. Some thirty-eight have passed away, including fifteen who were KIA in Vietnam. A regular newsletter has been created, and we have convened at reunion gatherings from time to time. It has taken a while, but I have discovered that the significance of my service time has steadily increased through the years to the point where I have come to treasure my association with this extraordinary group. Together, we persevered in the tempestuous 1960s and dared to fly in the face of popular opinion by becoming United States Marine officers. To a man, we were willing to put our lives on the line. Many of us did, and tragically, too many of us made the ultimate sacrifice.

It was a sprightly troop of B Company alumni and our ladies who assembled in platoon strength on a bright and sunny morning in mid-October 2016 in a large classroom at The Basic School in Quantico. (The meeting was set for 0930. It should have been at 0530, just for tradition's sake.) Delightfully, Elaine Zimmer was on hand. The Basic School's executive officer and protocol officer, Lieutenant Colonel Kevin Gallman and Major Dave Eagen, respectively, graciously briefed us on the state of the officer development program. Not only did we marvel at the current facilities and living spaces, but also how much the curriculum has been modified to adjust to a contemporary world. The staff even treats the students today like they are real officers instead of some sort of officer-aspirant candidates with no standing. There was a consensus in our group with no debate needed: we had it much tougher in our day, but then again, we were "the old Corps."

I for one was very impressed at the remarkable, healthy-looking young men and women students running around with hair trimmed short, robust physiques, and perfectly pressed utilities. I was frankly surprised when I asked Joyce if back in the day we looked like them. She promptly replied that we did. Hard to believe now.

There was a banquet on the final evening of the event, where Lieutenant General Ron Christmas, Retired, was the featured speaker. The general's remarks hit home on many fronts. The Lion dancers brought in by Hon Lee were also outstanding. Perhaps the most moving and meaningful part of that memorable evening was the "missing man" place setting and candle set for those three dozen or so of our classmates who are no longer with us. Physically they are gone, but there is no question that they live on in our hearts.

Until fairly recently, many of us were so preoccupied with everyday living that we had little time to reflect back on what the Marine Corps meant on a personal basis. Some of my seeming haste to exit the service can be explained by the context of the times back in the early 1970s. The Vietnam War had become extremely unpopular and was getting much more so. The sight of a man in uniform was enough to spark catcalls and ridicule on the street of cities such as Philadelphia, where I was based. In fact, on at least one occasion I was actually spit upon and called a "baby killer" by some unsavory individuals as I walked along the sidewalk. A patriot to the core, I have always been willing to serve my country as directed, but quite candidly, even I at that point had pretty much concluded as to the folly of our presence in Southeast Asia. Marines were dying, including some of my best friends. It was becoming more and more difficult to rationalize such things. I was pleased to have served in such a fine organization, but felt it was time to move on. For me, remaining a Marine to collect a paycheck made little sense.

I did keep in touch with some of my closer friends from the service but was mainly engrossed in earning a living and raising a family for some twenty years or so, until the Gulf War and ultimately 9/11 ignited a rejuvenated wave of patriotism that had never existed for "our" war. As if by magic, our men and women in uniform were transformed from the nefarious and nasty automatons that we had been labeled to bona fide national heroes. While global politics were still problematic at best, the general public embraced our troops with an enthusiasm that had not been seen since World War II. I was very gratified to observe that the man on the street actually had some appreciation for the personal sacrifices our military was making on his behalf. Service in our military was no longer an embarrassment or at best, a second-class occupation. You could actually wear a uniform in public without fear of disrespect and mockery. The tide of patriotism and nationalism that washed across our county has been wonderful to watch.

To some degree, the groundswell of support for our troops was perfectly understandable. The sheer horror of 9/11 on our own soil was observed firsthand by all Americans. Our very existence had been threatened from a mysterious enemy most of us had never even heard of. The threat was real and very close to home. In most people's judgement, swift military retribution was just, right, and appropriate. To the enormous appreciation of a grateful nation, our soldiers, sailors, and Marines willingly and gallantly went forward to protect us.

When Charlie, Jerry, and I were NROTC students at Brown in the 1960s, no such threat was apparent or imminent. I had no illusions of returning home from my Westpac tour as a conquering hero, but was not prepared for the ubiquitous scorn. Average Americans could not have cared less about the "domino theory" in Southeast Asia. Where? What theory? The massive casualty counts and scant prospects for a satisfactory resolution exacerbated the pervasive contempt for our involvement in such a mess so far away. Those feelings melded perfectly with the new age of liberalism to cast anyone and everyone associated with Vietnam in an unfortunate light, including us Marines. Heroes? Hell, we were viewed by many as a big part of the problem. An almost complete lack of appreciation for our unrequited efforts was profoundly disappointing.

As I think back on it now, maybe it isn't surprising that it took just about forty years until I received my very first "thank you for your service." It was unbelievably refreshing to hear that based upon the total opposite reaction we were confronted with from the general public in the 1960s. I never pass anyone in uniform when I don't shake their hand and express my heartfelt thanks for the sacrifices they are making. Having been on the opposite end of such treatment, I have a very good idea that they are very appreciative of such consideration, however small. Forty years was a long wait.

These days, with more time on my hands than constructive applications to use it, certain seemingly inconsequential, everyday events have grown to have special meaning for me. Blessed with almost a squad of grandchildren who are rapidly passing through their elementary school years, Marine Corps aside, November has become one of my favorite months. For several years running now I have been elated to have been asked to serve as a grandchild's "veteran" at school on Veteran's Day. Although I should have learned by now to "never volunteer," in these cases I do make an exception. I am deeply honored to be asked. Whether it is for a simple raising of the flag to taps or a panel discussion in front of twenty-five squirming second-graders, I extract much joy from those occasions. Yet I continue to ponder just what sort of world we are leaving for those kids. I sincerely hope our legacy to them is much better than what we inherited.

On Veteran's Day, November 11 last, at 0800, I was standing at attention (or maybe it was closer to a relaxed "parade rest") near the flagpole at the front of grandson Wyatt's sixth-grade school in Pearland, Texas. It was a typically humid and blustery fall day in south Texas. Accompanying me as honored guests were a motley group of some ten other veterans of various ages, conflicts, and service branches. The school had arranged for readings of original essays from several students, playing of the national anthem while raising of our flag, and taps, to be followed by "hot chow (doughnuts) on the high ground." As I shifted from foot to foot to ease my chronic arthritic back pain, I surveyed the throng of young faces obviously encompassing a variety of ethnic and racial backgrounds. Try as they might to conduct themselves with "event-appropriate" solemnity, their youthful vigor and boundless energy could hardly be contained.

As I stood there watching and listening to those children who truly represent our country's future, I happened to notice a Southwest Airlines 737 off in the distant sky on final approach to Hobby Airport, a few miles to the north. There was a sudden yank at my heartstrings. Had things turned out just a little bit differently, maybe my two good friends could have been in the cockpit guiding that commercial airliner in. As I struggled to maintain the composure befitting a "tough" Marine in front of all those kids, I was suddenly hammered by another thought. While I have never really understood why Charlie and Jerry, or for that matter, any of us, had to die, I have never felt anyone perished in vain. Nonetheless, for decades I have been searching for some reassurance in that regard.

Abruptly, miraculously, during the little ceremony that morning, there it was right in front of me: an epiphany, perhaps, those legions of screaming little kids. Indeed, our men's ultimate sacrifices have ensured that those youngsters, and millions of others like them, will have the opportunity to pursue free, bountiful, and wonderful lives that they enjoy. A tragic tradeoff to be sure, but I shudder to contemplate the alternative.

Semper fi.

SOURCES

~ 6

IN THE PREPARATION OF THIS book, the author has primarily relied on his own personal recollections, photographs, notes, and papers but also consulted with a number of other individuals and sources of information. A partial list includes:

1. The 108th edition of *Liber Brunensis*, which is the Brown University Class of 1966 yearbook
2. The website of Brown University, especially excerpts from Martha Mitchell's *Encyclopedia Brunonina*
3. Brooks, David, <u>The Road to Character,</u> Random House, New York; 2015
4. Elaine Zimmer Davis' "Bringing Jerry Home" website http://www.bringingjerryhome.com/
5. Official records as available on government websites including Command Chronology Reports
6. Interviews, discussion, and correspondence with members of USMC TBS-167, friends, and family members.

ABOUT THE AUTHOR

—⟋—

ROBERT JOHN. DELUCA IS A retired businessman, who holds BA and MBA degrees from Brown University and the University of Pittsburgh, respectively. A Captain in the United States Marine Corps, he served in Vietnam. After working in banking with the Mellon Bank in Pittsburgh and Citibank of New York, he eventually settled in Houston where he founded Desert Southwest Realty. His extensive business background provides a strong platform and fertile resource for his writing endeavors. He has raised a family of four sons, and resides with his awesome wife, grandchild-of-the-week, and bullmastiff in Friendswood, Texas.

His books include three novels: *The Pact with the Devil*, *The Sister Edith,* and the soon to be released *The Master of Deceit.* In addition to *Beatles, Books, Bombs, and Beyond* he has completed a non-fiction work, *The Perfect Pro Football Coach.* His website: http://bdlauthor.com/

Made in the USA
Middletown, DE
02 August 2017